W9-CCD-131

DISCARD

Soul Repair

SOUL REPAIR

Recovering from Moral Injury after War

Rita Nakashima Brock
and Gabriella Lettini

*With Camillo "Mac" Bica, Herman Keizer Jr.,
Pamela Lightsey, and Camilo Ernesto Mejía*

Beacon Press
Boston

Beacon Press
25 Beacon Street
Boston, Massachusetts 02108-2892
www.beacon.org

Beacon Press books
are published under the auspices of
the Unitarian Universalist Association of Congregations.

15   14   13   12   8   7   6   5   4   3   2   1

This book is printed on acid-free paper that meets the uncoated paper
ANSI/NISO specifications for permanence as revised in 1992.

Text design by Wilsted & Taylor Publishing Services

Brock, Rita Nakashima.
Soul repair : recovering from moral injury after war / Rita Nakashima Brock and
Gabriella Lettini ; with Camillo Mac Bica, Herman Keizer, Jr., Pamela Lightsey,
and Camilo Ernesto Mejia.
p. cm.
Includes bibliographical references.
ISBN 978-0-8070-2907-7 (hardcover : alk. paper)
1. Military ethics—United States. 2. War—Moral and ethical aspects.
3. Veterans—Mental health—United States. 4. Guilt and culture—United
States. 5. Remorse. 6. Shame—Moral and ethical aspects. 7. Veterans—
United States—Psychology. 8. Veterans—Suicidal behavior—United States—
Prevention. 9. Forgiveness—Therapeutic use. I. Lettini, Gabriella. II. Title.
III. Title: Recovering from moral injury after war.
U22.B734 2012
174'.9355—dc23   2012020733

IN MEMORIAM

Roy Grady Brock
1923–1976

Giuseppe Torelli
1979–2009

My father, who fought in World War II, tried to tell me, "War is not as glamorous as they make it out to be." But I was too stubborn and bull-headed to listen. When you are young, you want to get that experience for yourself . . . and, boy, I asked for it.

I saw more than I ever wanted to see. . . . You are seeing how war affects civilians in the area. Every house you look at has bomb craters or bullet holes in it. . . . It makes them put their humanity aside to make it in a war zone. You see all that stuff and you see how it affects you and everyone around you, and you say, "Why are we doing this anymore?"

[I found out] we were in the area of Iraq that was supposed to be the Garden of Eden, the cradle of civilization where mankind began. I had to ask myself, "Why am I carrying around an M16 in the Garden of Eden?"

KEVIN BENDERMAN, COMBAT VETERAN,
U.S. ARMY, IN *SOLDIERS OF CONSCIENCE*

Contents

Introduction

To violate your conscience
is to commit moral suicide.

REV. HERMAN KEIZER JR.,
Colonel and Chaplain, U.S. Army, Ret.

After we send men and women off to war, how do we bring them home to peace?

Obviously distraught, the three people huddled, whispering to each other while they waited patiently at the end of a long line that had formed after Rita's lecture on moral injury in Houston, Texas. When the two women and the man finally reached her, they said they were from a United Methodist Church. Their words tumbled out on top of each other: "You don't know how much your lecture meant to us . . . We didn't know how to help him . . . The suicide was such a shock . . . The whole church is heartbroken . . . We wish we had known about moral injury . . . It makes so much sense . . . Maybe we could have helped him."

The group's distress was raw and urgent. Their description was disjointed, as if their jumbled memories had not come into focus. When they realized that Rita was puzzled, they filled in some of the details. They explained that the suicide of a young veteran, deeply beloved in their church, was unexpected. The whole church community was reeling and struggling to understand how it had failed him. He was a hero to so many, they said, that the Department of Veterans Affairs (VA) had sent crisis counselors to a national gathering of veterans meeting at the time of the suicide. After the group explained the impact of the suicide on them and their community, one of the women said, "We want to learn more about moral injury. Our community needs this information. We couldn't save Clay, but maybe we can help save others."

Within days of Rita's lecture in April 2011, national media sources reported Clay Warren Hunt's story. He was a twenty-eight-year-old former marine corporal who earned a Purple Heart serving in Iraq and Afghanistan. He had been active in a suicide-prevention program for vets. Since 2009, he had been a model to other veterans of a successful return home. He married and started college in California; he advocated for veterans' rights and worked in disaster relief. He was being treated for post-traumatic stress disorder (PTSD). Then, his marriage ended, he left school, went into treatment for depression, and returned to Houston where he got a job and an apartment in Sugar Land, Texas. On March 31, 2011, he bolted himself in that apartment and shot himself. Over a thousand people attended his funeral.[1]

Veteran suicides average one every eighty minutes, an unprecedented eighteen a day or six thousand a year. They are 20 percent of all U.S. suicides, though veterans of all wars are only about 7 percent of the U.S. population. Between 2005 and 2007, the national suicide rate among veterans under age thirty *rose 26 percent*. In Texas—home of the largest military base in the world and the third-highest veteran population—*rates rose 40 percent* between 2006 and 2009. These rates continue, despite required mental health screenings of those leaving the military, more research on PTSD, and better methods for treating it. Veterans are also disproportionately homeless, unemployed, poor, divorced, and imprisoned. The statistics, however, do not disclose the devastating impact of war on veterans' families and friends, on their communities, and on other veterans.[2]

The journey home to peace is perilous after war. We can make it less lonely and lethal. The veterans' stories that unfold in this book describe a wound of war called "moral injury," the violation of core moral beliefs. The stories reveal the lifelong struggle of veterans to live with its scars, the impact on their families, and the various ways our society can support the recovery of those who experience moral injury.

Moral injury is not PTSD. Many books on veteran healing confuse and conflate them into one thing. It is possible, though, to have moral injury without PTSD. The difference between them is partly physical. PTSD occurs in response to prolonged, extreme trauma and is a fear-victim reaction to danger. It produces hormones that affect the brain's amygdala and hippocampus, which control responses to fear, as well as regulate emotions and connect fear to memory. A sufferer often has difficulty forming a coherent memory of a traumatic event or may even be unable to recall it. Symptoms include flashbacks, nightmares, hypervigilance, and dissociation.

Our ability to calm or extinguish fear and process emotions is often impaired by trauma, and a previous history of emotional trauma or a brain injury can make a person more susceptible to PTSD. Dissociative episodes can put sufferers back into experiences of terror and make them lose a sense of the present. They can feel unreasonable fear in ordinary situations or startle at sounds that mimic battle. They may experience a compulsive need to retell stories of terror, to reenact them, and to transfer past fear-inducing conditions to the present. With PTSD, memory erupts uncontrollably and retraumatizes the sufferer, which can make retrieving a coherent memory nearly impossible. Clinicians have treatments for PTSD, and such therapies are crucial for those diagnosed with it.

The moral questions emerge after the traumatizing symptoms of PTSD are relieved enough for a person to construct a coherent memory of his or her experience. We organize emotionally intense memories into a story in the brain's prefrontal cortex, where self-control, planning, reasoning, and decision making occur. The mind creates a pattern from memory fragments stored in various places. Emotions are essential to moral conscience, but until people can construct enough of a coherent narrative to grasp what they did, they cannot evaluate it. The brain organizes experiences and evaluates them, based on people's capacity to think about moral values and feel empathy at the same time.[3]

Marine veteran and philosopher Camillo "Mac" Bica used the term *moral injury* in his war journals from Vietnam, and, from the perspective both of warrior and of moral philosopher, he has explored the agony of this inner judgment against himself. Moral injury is the result of reflection on memories of war or other extreme traumatic conditions. It comes from having transgressed one's basic moral identity and violated core moral beliefs.

Moral injury names a deep and old dilemma of war. The moral anguish of warriors defines much literature about war from ancient times to the present, such as the Greek *Iliad* and Indian *Bhagavad-Gita*, both war epics; the Hebrew Psalms; and modern novels and films, such as *Catch-22*, *The Deer Hunter*, or *Matterhorn*. We see discussions of moral injury in current memoirs of the wars in Afghanistan and Iraq. In *Packing Inferno: The Unmaking of a Marine*, Tyler E. Boudreau, a veteran of Iraq and former Marine officer, reflects on the apparent inability of societies to learn from works of art and history about the torture that war inflicts on the souls of veterans. He concludes that societies have understood war only as much as they really wanted to learn about it and its deeper meaning.

Not everyone was so unable or unwilling to understand, Tyler notes. In *Mrs. Dalloway*, Virginia Woolf portrayed the suicidal anguish after World War I of Septimus Smith as if she were a veteran herself. Tyler reflects on her perceptive depiction:

> She was just a writer. That tells me, if nothing else, that the information was there. The capacity to know existed. It wasn't beyond human understanding. They weren't too primitive. If Virginia Woolf knew about combat stress, everybody else could have known, too. They did not know because they didn't want to know.[4]

Still, not even Tyler could face telling the truth about war. After he left the Corps, he worked as a Casualty Assistance Calls Officer (CACO), which required him to call the parents of wounded Marines. He could not bring himself to call soldiers' families and report honestly that, among the wounds they suffered, "your boy is coming home with a broken heart." Never once was he able to say it, and he regrets it still that he did not.[5]

Moral injury results when soldiers violate their core moral beliefs, and in evaluating their behavior negatively, they feel they no longer live in a reliable, meaningful world and can no longer be regarded as decent human beings. They may feel this even if what they did was warranted and unavoidable. Killing, torturing prisoners, abusing dead bodies, or failing to prevent such acts can elicit moral injury. Handling human remains can be especially difficult; for example, in 2004, Jess Goodell served in the Marine Corps' first Mortuary Affairs unit in Iraq, which required her to recover and process remains of fallen soldiers, including drawing their outlines where they had fallen, filling in missing parts in black. In her memoir, *Shade It Black: Death and After in Iraq*, she describes the devastating aftermath of this work of facing death every day. Seeing someone else violate core moral values or feeling betrayed by persons in authority can also lead to a loss of meaning and faith. It can even emerge from witnessing a friend get killed and feeling survivor guilt. In experiencing a moral conflict, soldiers may judge themselves as worthless; they may decide no one can be trusted and isolate themselves from others; and they may abandon the values and beliefs that gave their lives meaning and guided their moral choices. Recently, Veterans Affairs clinicians have begun to conceptualize moral injury as separate from PTSD and as a hidden wound of war.[6]

The consequences of violating one's conscience, even if the act was unavoidable or seemed right at the time, can be devastating. Responses include overwhelming depression, guilt, and self-medication through alcohol or drugs. Moral injury can lead veterans to feelings of worthlessness, remorse, and despair; they may feel as if they lost their souls in combat and are no longer who they were. Connecting emotionally to others becomes impossible for those trapped inside the walls of such feelings. When the consequences become overwhelming, the only relief may seem to be to leave this life behind.

The tired truism, "war is hell," is also true of its aftermath, but the aftermath can be endless. War has a goal and tours of duty that end; its torments are intense and devastating, but they are not perpetual. War offers moral shields of honor and courage. Its camaraderie bonds warriors together around a common purpose and extreme danger. War offers service to a larger cause; it stumbles on despair. On the other hand, moral injury feeds on despair. When the narcotic emotional intensity and tight camaraderie of war are gone, withdrawal can be intense. As memory and reflection deepen, negative self-judgments can torment a soul for a lifetime. Moral injury destroys meaning and forsakes noble cause. It sinks warriors into states of silent, solitary suffering, where bonds of intimacy and care seem impossible. Its torments to the soul can make death a mercy.

The suffering of moral injury is grounded in the basic humanity of warriors. That humanity lies deeper in them than its betrayal in war. They learned their ethical values first from their families, neighbors, schools, and religious and community organizations. Whether people are religious, spiritual, or secular, most of us are trained to respect others, to relate to a world bigger than ourselves, and to feel compassion for those who suffer. For many families, a military career is one way to embody core moral values like love of country and service to others.

When veterans return to our communities after war, we owe it to them and to ourselves to do our best to support their recovery. To do so, however, we must be willing to engage the same intense moral questions that veterans undertake about our own responsibility as a society for having sent them to war. This book is an invitation to accept that transformative process.

The military, which trains people to kill, also teaches moral values to all who serve. Soldiers are instructed in the principles of just war and the legal and ethical conduct of war, including the need to protect noncombatants and to refrain from torturing prisoners. People in the military often understand the principles of just war and international standards better than members of the religious and philosophical traditions that espouse them. Paradoxically, current military regulations require soldiers to fight all wars, regardless of their moral evaluations, which can create profound inner conflicts for them.

Combatants who support a war and serve willingly also experience moral injury because the actual conditions of war are morally anguishing. As every veteran of combat knows, the ideal of war service, the glamour of its heroics, and the training for killing fail to prepare warriors for its true horrors and moral atrocities. The wars in Iraq and Afghanistan, especially, present terrible moral dilemmas for engagement because the lines between civilians and combatants are invisible and because the absence of clear battle lines makes every situation potentially lethal. Even women, children, and family pets can be dangerous or used as shields. These category confusions are also moral confusions, and they are aggravated by the reflexive shooting methods the military started teaching after World War II: the training suppresses combatants' ability to exercise moral discernment before taking action. Many veterans recount with anguish stories about shooting reflexively at unarmed civilians in a split second, without making a conscious decision to take a life. In addition, many soldiers experience repeated exposure to these morally compromising situations through multiple deployments.

War's lingering phantoms haunt every society. In the bodies and souls of those who experience combat, war always comes home to the rest of us. Veterans' families and communities, especially, carry these burdens. While the suicide rate is especially high among the veterans of the current wars, suicide still bedevils the eighteen million combat veterans in the United States. For the country has sent its forces into war nearly every year since 1945. During the years of the war in Vietnam, conscription and public resistance to the conflict traumatized the entire generation that reached adulthood between 1964 and 1975.

In many traditional societies, all returning soldiers were required to undergo a period of ritual purification and rehabilitation before re-entering their ordinary lives after war. For example, the Navajo people of the Southwest developed a ceremonial process called 'Anaa 'jí, or "the Enemy Way," which was used to cure sickness that came from contact with a deceased non-Navajo, participation in war, fatal accidents, and other encounters with death, such as corpses and graves. Some forms of it took almost two weeks to complete. Its adaptation to modern times is used to reintegrate veterans of combat serving in the U.S. armed services and is supported by VA health professionals. In another example, Christian churches in the first millennium required anyone who "shed human blood" to undergo a rehabilitation process that included reverting to the status of someone who had not yet been baptized and was undergoing training in Christian faith. Now long in disuse, this ancient form of quarantine was required because early Christians understood that killing or participating in war, regardless of the reasons, injured the souls of those who fought. Returning soldiers were commonly expected to spend at least a year among the order of penitents.[7]

Whether we support or oppose a particular war, we contribute to a better, more moral society when we take responsibility for healing the devastating aftermath of combat. To accept responsibility requires people courageous enough to face the moral questions that war raises and people willing to listen compassionately and carefully to the moral anguish of veterans.

As the authors of this book, one an immigrant from Italy and the other an immigrant from Japan, we have been deeply affected by moral injury through combat veterans in our families. While neither of us is a veteran, we, like many millions of people, were born and raised under the shadow of war. As we relate below, we have also been deeply affected by our work with veterans today,

Gabriella

Gabriella grew up in Turin, also the hometown of Primo Levi, who wrote some of the most harrowing accounts of the effects of war on the human spirit. Recently, her cousin, a young southern Italian veteran who had participated in several humanitarian missions abroad, took a leave for depression. While on leave and without warning, he tried to kill his mother and then killed himself. His death was but one tragedy in her family's long legacy of war.

Gabriella's maternal family lived near Turin in the Cottian Alps of northern Italy on the border with France, where antifascism and war resistance during World War II were very strong. Three generations of women in her family talked incessantly about "the war." Some stories were told to all; others were spoken in hushed tones, not for children to hear. The men said less in public, but they often gathered in veterans' circles.

In 1943, Nazi forces occupied Italy. Gabriella's grandmother Giulia and her older brother Albert joined the Resistance, motivated both by their Waldensian Protestant faith and their communist beliefs. They were in their mid-twenties and took the combat names of Franca and Ivo. Giulia already had five children; she placed them in different living situations until the end of the war. One of the younger girls was sent to stay with a family in Switzerland. The brothers stayed with Giulia's mother Rachele and witnessed Nazi soldiers threatening to kill her because she would not disclose where her children were hiding. The Nazis burned their house to the ground. A partially damaged Bible was saved from the fire, which Gabriella's great-grandmother Rachele gave to her as she was leaving to attend the Waldensian seminary in Rome. Gabriella's mother was left in an orphanage for two years, and to this day, she claims no one explained what was happening to her or visited her there. Her fears of abandonment and difficulties in social relationships pose a constant challenge for her daughters. Gabriella says,

> War was one of the main narratives of my upbringing. Even decades later, I keep discovering untold stories, layers of trauma, and invisible wounds that still inform the complex dynamics of my troubled family history and therefore of who I am today.
>
> In Italy, everyone had direct experience of WWII, even women

and children. When I was growing up in the seventies, war stories were still told everywhere: at family reunions, in church, in casual store conversations, in school curricula, in the books we were given to read.

My grandmother Giulia was jailed on a couple of occasions. Her brother Albert was captured in '44, and in January of 1945, he was sent to the concentration camp of Mauthausen, just months before the end of the war. A political prisoner whose skills as a mechanic were in demand, he survived. He spoke proudly of having been a Partisan, but shared very little about Mauthausen. He used to explain, cryptically and not unlike Primo Levi, that only the worst people survived the camps. No one really dared to ask what he meant.

In spring 2011, Albert shot himself in the head at eighty-eight. He was in good health for his age, had a comfortable financial situation, and good family relationships.

In the hours after hearing about Albert's death, as I was trying to make some sense of the news, I did a simple search online about him. To my surprise, I found the transcripts of a very long interview that Albert granted in 1982 for an oral history research project for a Resistance archive that had only been publicly available online since 2009.

With the simple and direct language of a man who came from generations of peasants and was never formally educated, Albert shared with his interviewer stories and thoughts that had never circulated in the family. When he started to see glimpses of the atrocities committed in Mauthausen, the full scope of which he fully realized only after the camp was liberated, his first reaction was to consider suicide: he thought about running toward the gates so he could be shot. Then, suddenly, an irresistible desire to live took hold of him. Albert wanted to survive, whatever it took.

One particular story kept haunting me. When the Allied forces were bombing the camp, Albert was regularly sent to hide in some trenches near his barrack because he was considered among the valuable labor force:

They made us go there to find shelter. . . . [I]t's not that they really wanted to protect us, but only because we were like a machine they needed at that moment. When it rained it got very muddy . . . but then we did not want to go there anymore. . . . [T]hey were throwing ashes in those trenches, and we did not want to go there any longer because we knew that in those ashes there were our comrades that had been killed. They were the ashes from the cremation chambers . . . and the stench, this stench from the cremation chambers, you could smell it.

He had to find shelter, at twenty, awash in the ashes of the thousands who had been exterminated that day. I cannot know for sure what pushed Albert to shoot himself. But I do know that people who witness and fail to prevent atrocities experience moral injury. "The worst survive," Albert used to tell us. For sure, the guilt and the horror stayed with him for the rest of his life. And we did not dare to ask about it.

Rita

Rita was born in 1950 to a Japanese mother in Fukuoka, Japan, a city just two hours from Nagasaki by train. Like other families in occupied Japan, Rita's natal family struggled to rebuild their lives after the war. Her mother, Ayako Nakashima, gave up her ambition to be a teacher and trained as a nurse with the Red Cross. Rita's birth father, a Puerto Rican in the U.S. Army, was sent to Korea when Rita was six months old. She was never told about him and did not learn of him until her mother died in 1983. Ayako worked in the U.S. Army hospital in Fukuoka, and, when Rita was two, she met and married Roy Brock, a veteran of World War II, a medic, and a career soldier. Because Rita learned English at the age of six, when Roy was ordered to Fort Riley, Kansas, she came to know him well only after they shared a language. But once they were in the United States, the two became very close as he encouraged her transition to American life, raising her to read great writers, to study art, and to attend Protestant chapel services on the base.

Rita grew up eavesdropping on her father's card games with other soldiers, which was when they drank beer, smoked Camels, and told stories of World War II. She noticed that Roy's stories of battles kept changing, as if his memory were faulty or he were making things up and forgot what he'd said. Sometimes he seemed to borrow details from other men's stories. She suspected he lied much of the time, and, because he was otherwise an honest person, she wondered why he lied.

In 1966, Roy was sent to California's arid Mojave Desert to train for the soggy jungles of Vietnam. Roy did two tours as the head of a field medical aid station, and throughout his time away, he sent cassette-tape messages to Rita and her mother. In recordings to Rita, he often began a story with, "Don't tell your mother, I don't want to worry her." As if his tales would not worry his sixteen-year-old daughter.

Rita learned that Roy had received a reprimand for refusing to carry a gun. Then, Roy had run into a minefield and carried his wounded commanding officer to safety, which meant he was allowed to remain unarmed with impunity. He also did other unauthorized things, like providing medical services to Vietnamese civilians in the area. He described a young Vietnamese woman, the same age as Rita, whom he recruited to be his guide. She led him through the jungle to villages in the hills whenever he could leave his medic station in the hands of an assistant. Roy passed out antibiotics and painkillers to the sick and treated wounds among the injured. He spoke at length about the young guide's intelligence, strength, and agility, her capacities for endurance, and her moral character and resolve to help her people.

Roy returned home in the fall of 1968 after his second tour, totally disillusioned and disheartened and a different father from the one who left in 1966. Announcing that "the Army today is not this man's Army, not what I signed up for," he retired a year short of thirty years, rather than stay in military service another minute. He became controlling with his children and uncommunicative, preferring to spend hours alone. In his fierce need to curtail Rita's newfound freedom in college, he and she had a major physical fight that broke their relationship. She refused to live at home after that incident.

Not until many years after Roy died did Rita understand what had happened to him in World War II and Vietnam. She learned from her younger sister that he had been captured early in his time in World War II and was in a POW camp. When he was sent stateside, Walter Reed Hospital doctors gave him electroshock treatments and shipped him home in a near-catatonic state to Caledonia, Mississippi. Roy's cousin Virginia Ann, who was the person he was closest to growing up, fleshed out this story in detail when Rita visited her in July 2011. The conversation began because Rita was explaining her work on moral injury in veterans:

> Virginia Ann told me that when Roy came home from the war, he shook all the time. The family didn't know what was wrong with him and worried whether he would ever be all right. But, because her mother had epilepsy, she said, "We were kinda used to having someone around who wasn't all there all the time. We just took care of him and let him be." It took him over a year to rally, but Virginia Ann suspects he had lost most of his memory. They never got much out of him about his war experience: "Makes you wonder, what happened to him that was so awful."
>
> But there was another POW in Caledonia, and Virginia Ann had heard him give a talk about his experiences, which she suspects were like Roy's: "The guy told us that the prisoners were kept in the open, in pens like animals. They wore their uniforms until they rotted off their bodies. The Germans didn't give them clothes—hell, they hardly even fed them. They were so hungry they'd eat just 'bout anything, grass or tree bark. It was awful. The guy said once he watched two soldiers fighting over a cricket, they were so hungry."
>
> What Virginia Ann said next shocked me. "You know," she

reflected, "Vietnam was real hard on your daddy, maybe worse than the first war. I don't think he ever got over what they did to that Vietnamese girl he knew. I think she was like a guide or informant or something like that."

"What happened to her?" I asked.

Some soldiers had captured her. Then, they tortured, raped, and killed her. Roy found the body. "I know he was pretty broken up inside and disgusted with those men. He never wanted to see them again or stay in the Army. He just couldn't stand what happened to her," Virginia Ann told me.

From the time he was eighteen until he was forty-five, Roy served as an enlisted man doing work he found important and meaningful. He served in two wars and survived. And then, his fellow soldiers tortured and murdered a young Asian woman the age of his own Asian daughter, a woman he may have placed in harm's way by befriending her. He never got over it.

I try to imagine what he might have felt when he found that body, but I know I've never experienced anything that devastating. Looking back to when he came home, I understand now why the two of us had such a harrowing struggle over my independence, why he became suddenly so fierce about controlling me. He couldn't save her, so he had to save me, perhaps. I'll never know fully why he did what he did, but I have forgiven him, and I regret he died so soon of a heart attack, while we were still estranged.

OUR FAMILY EXPERIENCES have made us especially attuned to the cost of sending people to war, even when fighting may have been necessary. When we met nearly a decade ago, we found we shared a commitment to many ethical issues related to poverty, injustice, and violence. As the Afghanistan and Iraq wars escalated, we wondered how young veterans were coping with the aftermath of combat in Iraq and Afghanistan. We knew that the Vatican, most Protestant denominations, moral philosophers, and a number of other religious leaders and groups had declared the war in Iraq unjust and in violation of international laws. We were searching for some approach to moral questions of war that went deeper than the ideologically polarized pro-war versus pacifist positions that characterized many debates about war. In addition, public opinion turned against the war in 2005, and as professors in higher education, we were concerned about the impact of the wars on a new generation of young adults. We believe that most moral decisions are based on relationships and empathy for those affected and that the most difficult decisions happen in morally complex situations with competing demands and contradictory principles. We agreed that protests against the war and moral arguments against it were not enough. We were also concerned about the alarming rates of veteran suicides, especially veterans under thirty years old.

In the winter of 2008, we met with documentary filmmakers, Catherine Ryan and Gary Weimberg of Luna Productions, who had created *Soldiers of Conscience*, an Emmy-nominated film that had touched us both deeply. It follows eight soldiers who fought in Iraq, four of whom believed they had done the right thing and four who chose to apply for conscientious objector status after their first deployment. In showing how all eight had weighed moral questions, we realized that hearing the moral voices of veterans about their war service was important, not only for nuancing debates about the wars in Afghanistan and Iraq, but also for helping the public understand society's responsibility for them and how soldiers struggle with conscience in war. We learned that it was easy to use our own moral position on a war as a defensive barrier that closed our hearts to the kind of deep listening that transformed us.

We thought that a Truth Commission on Conscience in War (TCCW) might be a helpful approach to putting the moral issues before the public. We each had experiences with previous truth commissions as researchers of their processes and as organizers of them. We believed they opened people to truth in unique ways and enabled a deep quality of listening that is rare in society. In planning the TCCW, we learned that many veterans, regardless of their moral position on the war they fought, struggle with moral conscience after fighting. We heard from veterans who served willingly, believing the wars to be just, and others who opposed the wars. We wanted to encourage conversations about war across lines of difference, so that people might work together to support moral conscience in veterans and those serving in the military.

When we began the two years of work it took to create the Truth Commission, we did not know what would result from testimonies of such a range of combat veterans. In addition to the veterans, we heard from a VA psychiatrist, a legal expert on conscientious objection, three religious leaders—Jewish, Christian, and Muslim—who explained the criteria for the moral conduct of war from their traditions, and a seasoned war correspondent who described the impact of war on soldiers and societies. We invited a wide range of leaders to be commissioners, some of whom affirmed military service, others who were veterans, others who advocated just war and believed it was seldom used adequately before the rush to war, and still others who were pacifists. The public hearing in March 2010 at the Riverside Church in New York presented fourteen witnesses and drew five hundred members of the public.[8]

As we listened intently to powerful testimonies for three hours, the moral weight of what we heard moved us deeply. On the day following the public hearing, the seventy-five truth commissioners and fourteen testifiers met in private to discuss what we had heard and what we wanted to recommend. As part of the preparation for this meeting, we asked the commissioners to read the new VA research on moral injury, which was extremely helpful to us in understanding the testimony we heard. The testifiers and commissioners recommended unanimously that our communities should learn more about moral injury. In the wake of that recommendation, the two of us and Rev. Herman Keizer Jr., host of the TCCW and in military service for forty years, worked to create a center for soul repair to further research, deepen understanding, and offer education about moral injury. We have received support and encouragement from many others who participated in the Truth Commission. In June 2012, the Soul Repair Center became a reality at Brite Divinity School in Fort Worth, Texas.

Three years ago, we could not have imagined how much we would learn, where this work would take us, or how far our network of friends would expand. In the following pages, you will find insights about the moral struggle of veterans from some we have come to know through the film and the TCCW. In addition, four of the veterans who testified at the Truth Commission, Camillo "Mac" Bica, Herman Keizer Jr., Pamela Lightsey, and Camilo Mejía have generously offered their stories for this book, so that others might understand more fully the cost of serving in war. In Pamela's story, we learn what it means to be a military veteran with a son serving in Iraq. We invite you on a journey through these pages that will change your life, as it has changed ours.

1

I Became a Soldier

> War has been part of my life virtually
> for as long as I can remember.
> CAMILLO C. "MAC" BICA, philosopher
> of war, former U.S. Marine Captain, and
> Vietnam veteran

People in military service are our neighbors; they are the beloved
sons and daughters, fathers and mothers, sisters and brothers, aunts
and uncles, and cousins of ordinary people. Their reasons for being
in the military are as unique and diverse as the various people they
leave behind in civilian life. But serving in the armed forces changes
them.

Military service for most of American history was widely regarded
as a sign of strength of character and an expression of patriotism.
With the GI Bill of 1944–1956, two-and-a-half-million war veterans
bought homes, and the education benefit created a vast number of
college-educated men, including over a dozen Nobel laureates, two
dozen Pulitzer Prize winners, three Supreme Court justices, and three
U.S. presidents. The education benefit had a negative impact on civilian women's access to higher education and was not as useful to black

men in the south, but it was a major builder of the middle class that grew after World War II. Without that postwar middle class, the social progress for women, students, and minorities that marked the 1960s to the 1980s would have been much more difficult. Change came with the Vietnam War. The public's objections to the war and vehement opposition to the draft changed attitudes toward military service. It became suspect in most liberal circles, but it continued to enhance many American men's careers.[1]

A commission to a military academy still delivers a first-rate education, and, even among the enlisted ranks, a desire for a college education is a major reason for joining the military. Many who enlisted immediately after the terrorist attacks of September 11, 2001, wanted to defend their country. Others had joined before the attacks and were prepared to fight, though they may not have expected to. Many soldiers with moral misgivings about the Iraq War fought anyway because of their loyalty to their unit, because of the close friends they did not want to abandon, and because military service required it. Others deployed because a career in the military is greatly enhanced by combat experience.

The end of the draft in 1974 created a perception that military service is totally voluntary, but the term "voluntary" needs interrogation. It oversimplifies why people join the military. A study in 2007 found that troops who died in Iraq were disproportionately poorer than the rest of Americans, what some people have chosen to call a "poverty draft." The numbers are significant: almost three-fourths of U.S. troops in Iraq were from towns where per capita income fell below the national average and over half were from communities where poverty levels were above the national average. Military recruiters, driven by quotas, work in offices found in poorer areas of cities, and new Army recruits come primarily from lower- to middle-class communities, southern states, and black, Hispanic, and Asian communities, according to official U.S. Army data. These numbers reflect Army special projects, such as "Hispanic H2 Tour" or the "Takin' It to the Streets Tour" to encourage the enlistment of Hispanic and African

American youth. In neighborhoods with high crime levels or in unstable or abusive families, military service may offer greater safety and what one man termed, "'three hots and a cot,' food and shelter where they can't turn you away." Recruiters, often through access to public schools, have been known to target children under age seventeen, sometimes as young as eleven, for military recruitment; this practice, according to a 2008 ACLU report, violates the United Nations Optional Protocol on Children in Armed Conflict.[2]

Joshua Casteel signed up in 1997 for the Delayed Enlistment Program during his junior year of high school and attended basic training the following summer. An evangelical son of ministers, a Republican, and a member of a military family with a long history of service in war, he attended West Point for a few months, but found its military rigidity constricting. Basic training had made him uncomfortable because his Christian upbringing did not prepare him for the chants: "Kill! Kill! Kill, without mercy, Sergeant!" and "Blood! Blood! Bright red blood, Sergeant!" He concluded he was better suited to a liberal arts college, where he studied the history of Christian just war and pacifism. He also didn't care for the college ROTC regimen any more than the rigidity of West Point, so his commitment to the military was beginning to fade until the attacks of 9/11. When he deployed to Iraq in 2004, he felt a need to fulfill his duty as a soldier because he had sworn to do so.

Military service defined love of country in Kevin Benderman's family. He was born in Alabama and raised there and in Tennessee, where his father had deep roots in the Southern Baptist tradition. In the Murray County Courthouse in Tennessee, an ancestor named Benderman is listed as fighting in the American Revolution. His grandfathers fought in World War I, his father in World War II, and his uncle in Korea. His older brother would have fought in Vietnam, but Kevin's father, who had earned a Purple Heart in France, kept him out because he did not want his sons to fight in war. Kevin suspects that war was a shock to him as a young religious man from rural Tennessee, and he wanted to spare his son, but until Kevin was in the Army, his father never spoke of his war experiences.

Despite his father's warnings, Kevin felt there was no higher honor than to serve his country and defend the values that established it. He was eager to take his turn at serving in war. At age twenty-two, he joined the military and, during his time at Fort Leavenworth, Kansas, in 1988, he witnessed the training of Iraqi officers in Saddam Hussein's army and the sale of weapons, conventional and chemical, to Iraq. He served for four years until 1991, and though he was called up to deploy during the Persian Gulf War, it ended before he was sent. He thought at the time about what he had seen earlier in Fort Leavenworth: "I remember thinking to myself how odd this was—to be training the officers of the Iraqi Army and then to be fighting them not two years later." He objected to how some of his fellow soldiers were treated, so he left the Army in 1991. In 2000, he reenlisted, starting over as a private, and in 2002, after training in the Army's Primary Leadership Development Course, he graduated at the top of a class of four hundred soldiers and became a sergeant. He was deployed to Iraq at the end of March 2003.[3]

When he turned sixteen, Tyler Boudreau went into a recruiting station to become a Marine. He was told to return when he was seventeen. Tyler, who was working at a tire store in a dangerous part of Boston, was required by his high school to watch the movie *Gallipoli*, which he suspects was supposed to challenge any student's idealization of war. But instead, Tyler loved the movie. He went back to see it dozens of times and eventually bought a copy of it. From a poor and abusive family, Tyler was looking for a way to prove himself and escape a dead-end job. He returned exactly a year to the day of his first attempt to enlist. Still suspicious of all authority figures, he read all the fine print in the contract carefully and tried to ask questions about the many points that did not make sense to him. "Just sign the fucking thing!" the recruiter roared.[4]

Each of the veterans who shares his or her story below reveals the complex reasons people enter the military. All, however, were changed forever by war. While the VA research on moral injury is new, the experience of moral injury in war is ancient. It haunts the lives of former soldiers.

Mac

Camillo "Mac" Bica, a Marine veteran and a philosopher who focuses on social/political theory and ethics, particularly as they relate to war, has struggled with moral injury since he fought in Vietnam. He is still active in the veteran community and meets regularly with fellow vets.

We first encountered Mac from articles he had written discussing the Iraq War at online sites such as *Truthout* and *AlterNet*. His perspective was passionate and poignant, and his analysis was razor sharp. Always, we heard a deep humanity in his voice. Mac is a veteran who volunteered for service in war and is not an absolute pacifist; he is rather a cogent proponent of just war. Because of his experience and his clear moral voice, we were convinced that he should testify at the Truth Commission on Conscience in War, and he accepted our invitation.

When we met him in March 2010 at the Riverside Church public hearing, we discovered that he is a powerful, compelling speaker. In addition, he is a poet of war who speaks with the heart of a warrior. His high forehead is ringed by a receding shock of gray hair, matched in color by his close-cropped beard. He has the serious, intelligent countenance of a philosopher, but a grave, sad look haunts his deep-set hazel eyes.

As a child, Mac grew up in Brooklyn on a diet of John Wayne movies, Roman Catholic education, and patriotism. He was deeply fascinated, even exhilarated, by the idea of war. He believed it was his duty to follow President Kennedy's admonition, "ask what you can do for your country." His parents were immigrants from Sicily who were grateful to live in the United States. His mother worked as a seamstress in a sweatshop. His father had served in World War II, believing that if he fought, his son would never have to.

As a child, Mac sometimes hid behind his family's green couch and eavesdropped on his father and other family members as they spoke about their experiences in combat while playing cards in a thick fog of Di Nobili cigar smoke and drinking *caffè corretto*, espresso "corrected" with grappa liquor. The men, Sicilian immigrants drafted into the U.S. military, were veterans of World War II and Korea. Mac's father was sent back to fight in Sicily, the land of his birth, where he served as a U.S. Army interpreter. Hidden behind that couch, Mac heard his father recount the devastation that the American forces had inflicted on the villages he had known as a child. Mac also heard about the guilt and shame his father felt for the deaths of so many innocent people who had been his neighbors. Mac also listened to many dramatic stories of adrenaline-charged close encounters with snipers and kamikaze attacks. But a story that made a profound impression on him was hearing his normally austere uncle Joe describe, with tears in his eyes, how he gently held a fellow Marine in his arms as he gasped his last breath at the frozen Chosin Reservoir in Korea. Mac was deeply moved to see such tenderness in this tough man.

Mac could not make sense of how war could be so fascinating and yet so devastating. He wanted to ask questions, but he instinctively realized that his father and his fellow veterans could only speak their truths about war to those who had shared similar experiences. Their smoky, grappa-anointed circle was their sanctuary.

While attending college, Mac enlisted in the Marine Corps Platoon Leader Candidate Program when he was seventeen. His goal was to become an educator, a position that would entitle him to a deferment from military service. His parents believed he should accept the deferment and could do so with dignity because his teaching was service to his society. After passing the licensing exams to teach in a public school, he was offered a position in the inner-city school where he had been a student teacher.

One of Mac's close childhood friends, Ralphie, had been killed in Vietnam just after turning nineteen. His parents had received a few fragments of bone and sinew and a letter from the President expressing regret for their loss and gratitude for Ralphie's sacrifice for freedom and democracy. It made Mac wonder how he could live with himself or face Ralphie's parents, should he accept the deferment.

Staying home, while so many of his generation were dying in Vietnam, felt cowardly. And so in 1968, after graduating from college, Mac accepted a commission as a Second Lieutenant in the United States Marine Corps.

Herm

Another veteran of Vietnam, Herman Keizer Jr., spent forty years in military service before retiring. He grew up in Chicago in a family of Dutch ancestry that belonged to the Christian Reformed Church in North America, a denomination he still serves.

When we were first planning the Truth Commission, we knew that having the right leadership at the public hearing would be important. We struggled to find the appropriate person to serve as the honorary host, someone who would understand what we wanted to achieve and who could speak at the occasion with credibility and gravitas. Several people, including a retired superintendent of West Point, mentioned a retired Army colonel and chaplain, Herm Keizer, who had worked for a long time to expand the regulations governing conscientious objection. Herm wanted them expanded beyond the narrow limits that required objection to all wars. He thought they should include the objections to a *particular* war because so many soldiers belong to religious traditions that follow ideas of just war, not pacifism. Herm accepted our invitation to serve as honorary host. He delivered a powerful opening speech and hosted the commission exactly as we imagined the ideal host would do.

Given what we had heard about Herm and his distinguished credentials and military medals, we expected someone who would convey a grave authority and have an air of sanctity, someone we would feel compelled to call "Chaplain Keizer." Instead, we met a man who was affable and laughed heartily; it was easy to call him Herm. Short and stocky with a ring of close-cropped salt-and-pepper hair and dark bushy eyebrows punctuated by warm brown eyes, his good cheer and ease attracts friends. But his hearty sense of humor masks a passionate seriousness when he talks about war and its moral consequences. He has radar for the trauma lying beneath the surface of stray comments from veterans, and an attentive, caring capacity to elicit their stories. Sometimes, when he speaks of his years as a military chaplain and the men and women he served, a somber look flashes behind his gaze like a distant thunderstorm.

Herm's family taught him strong values of family, faith, and service to God and country. He had three uncles who served in the Army in World War II. The third, his father's youngest brother, saw a lot of action in Europe. Herm remembers:

> He suffered shell shock and often would have very bad dreams. I remember going to his house with my dad after his wife called for help. Once we took a small German pistol from him, a .22 caliber, with no trigger housing and an elongated trigger. You could hide it in the palm of your hand, get close enough to an enemy, fire, and kill. Another time we found him on the floor with a bayonet, jabbing it into the floor to help him crawl. Those were frightening things for a young man to experience.

After high school, Herm enrolled at Calvin College in Grand Rapids, Michigan. When his third year ended, he lacked the funds to finish, so he had to take time off. He lost his deferment and was drafted in 1962.

Pamela

Pamela Lightsey followed her oldest brother into U.S. military service, married a fellow soldier, and is the mother of a veteran of the Iraq War. While she wrote a doctoral thesis on African and African American understandings of just war, she prayed for her son in Iraq and his safe return, knowing that they both believed it to be an unjust and immoral war. During this period, when she was a doctoral student, she and Rita met through a United Methodist scholarship program that supported women of color earning doctorates in a field that qualified them for seminary teaching. When the Truth Commission needed diverse clergy to testify to just war traditions, Rita immediately thought of Pamela, who delivered a compelling, thoughtful testimony at Riverside Church.

Pamela grew up in the Palm Beach area of Florida, one of seven children of Lillie Mae and Eddie Lee Lightsey. She inhabits the pulpit with a commanding presence, speaks with the passion and literary power of her Pentecostal roots in the black church, and has the inviting presence of someone at home in her own skin. Now the Associate Dean for Community Life and Lifelong Learning and Clinical Assistant Professor of Contextual Theology and Practice at Boston University School of Theology, she traveled a long journey to get there.

Pamela remembers her father, who grew up under the Jim Crow laws that mandated segregation, reminding his children when they drove by a particular tree near the police station that it was "a hanging tree," which meant the tree had been used to lynch black people. Eddie Lee Lightsey worked as a day laborer and truck driver; he often left home in the early mornings to stand on the street corner in hopes of someone needing work done that day. By juggling several jobs, he was able to bring groceries home and pay rent on his family's tiny two-bedroom apartment. He also had alcoholic binges in which he would beat his wife when her insults to his manhood pushed him beyond his limits.

Lillie Mae Lightsey was a maid for much of her life and a tough survivor. She used subversive means, such as contaminating food, to resist racist treatment from some of the white women who employed her. As Pamela reports:

> Mostly, my mother always tried to get paid properly for the work she was required to do. When she was dying of breast cancer, we were making calls trying to get her employers—rich and living in Palm Beach—to pay her last check. They refused, citing she "failed to come to work." How could she work while lying in the hospital? I will never forget that last indignity. If you—the final

employers of Lille Mae Lightsey who died in 1985—are still living, you should know at least one of her children remembers the
caliber of person you were and I will not let you absolve yourself
through gallant feats of white liberalism.

Pamela spent her young adult years as a zealous member of the
Pentecostal Church of God denomination, vigorously condemning
her older brother for being gay. He had come out as a gay man in his
teens, before, as Pamela says, "being out was cool." Within a few years,
she found the church's answers to her questions about the Bible and
how to live a faithful life as a woman were inadequate or illogical. She
grew to regret her homophobic behavior.

> I fell in love with the United Methodist Church because I could
> always ask the tough questions, and even if no one had the answer,
> they didn't play games with my faith. The members at the UM
> church I joined let me ask the questions and even had a few ques-
> tions for me. . . . And no one put me out of the church, no one
> "silenced" me, no one forbade me to use my mind, no one called
> me "reprobate" because of the courage to ask the tough questions
> of life that were unresolved by a literal reading of the text. They
> understood the logic against a literal reading and the danger of
> such interpretations.

Pamela's brother was an unlikely soldier. She is sure that many
of his military comrades knew he was gay, but he had such musical
talents for the military band—he served as an arranger, conductor,
bassoon-flute-oboe-piccolo player, and all-around musician—that he
successfully completed his term of enlistment. He didn't make the
military a career, moving on to other work after he left, but he appreciated his time in the military.

Pamela's motivation for joining the military was largely money.
The recruiter told her that the military would pay for her college education. Impatient to get that education, she joined, but what the recruiter did not tell her was that she would have to wait for the military

to decide when she went to school. She felt the misleading information she received was a breach of trust, a kind of lie that turned her off to the idea of a military career. She left military service within a few years, even though her husband stayed in.

Pamela worked in civil service during her husband's military career, moving with him to various postings in the United States and abroad. Her work in data processing required her to have a security clearance, as did some of her logistics work in the areas of transportation and supply. In her last position, Pamela helped procure javelin training equipment, night war-training equipment, and supplies to construct a lab where soldiers trained for various urban warfare situations. She completed college while she worked at Fort Benning, Georgia, and raised their daughter and son. Her marriage ended in divorce after almost sixteen years, and she went to seminary.

Pamela's son, Dweylon, had been an honor-roll student much of his childhood. He was more sophisticated and culturally literate than his peers because of his military upbringing, the education he had received at military base schools, and the crosscultural experiences he'd had at his father's overseas postings. When Pamela decided to move from Columbus, Georgia, near Ft. Benning, to do graduate work at the Interdenominational Theological Center in Atlanta, Dweylon asked if he might be allowed to live with his father in a nearby suburb. Wanting her son to have the benefit of more time with his father, Pamela agreed to let Dweylon stay with his father on weekdays and with her on weekends. This arrangement worked well until Dweylon's father remarried.

As Dweylon went through puberty, he, like many teenagers, became rebellious. The son Pamela sent to live with his father was soon in deep trouble. Within a year of living mostly with his dad, Dweylon had been expelled from high school. Given the impact of his father's remarriage on her son and his challenges with puberty, Pamela made a rapid decision to bring her son back to live with her full-time as she completed her masters of divinity degree. She enrolled him in a GED program to ensure that he continued in school and earned the equivalent of a high school diploma. Consistent with his earlier academic achievements, Dweylon did not stay long in the program because he easily passed all the required tests. Though he had been expelled in his junior year, Dweylon received his GED a year earlier than he would have received his diploma had he stayed in high school.

At the time Dweylon graduated, Pamela was working for the United Methodist Church, but she realized that she wanted a greater intellectual challenge and felt called to teach seminarians. She applied to Garrett-Evangelical Theological Seminary's doctor of philosophy program in theology and ethics and received scholarship support from the distinguished United Methodist Women of Color Scholars Program.

Pamela prepared to move to Chicago to begin as pastor of a thriving church in South Chicago and as a doctoral student at Garrett in Evanston, north of Chicago, which meant another move for Dweylon. As Dweylon reports, having already lost focus, he soon began to hang around with the wrong people. He stopped preparing for college and was earning no income. Rather than move with Pamela to Chicago, he asked her permission to join the military. She thought his request was simply another act of rebellion. Reluctantly, she agreed to it, believing that military life would help him refocus and teach him the discipline needed to go to college. Just shy of turning eighteen years old, and a few months before Pamela's departure for Chicago, Dweylon joined the Army.

The military had been his family's world during much of Dweylon's childhood and early adolescence, so it may also have been a return to a world he knew, rather than a move to a strange new city. When Pamela went to his graduation from basic training, Dweylon had excelled as a squad leader, even calling cadence during the ceremony. She realized that he was doing well in the military and was proud of him.

Camilo

We first encountered Camilo Ernesto Mejía in the documentary *Soldiers of Conscience*. His interviews in the film affected us deeply. In his understated, searching way, Camilo exhibited moral courage, honesty, and depth of thought. A short man with a strong presence, he has an open, intelligent face, a clear-eyed gaze, and a moral gravity that made his account of shooting a young man without having a memory of firing his gun profoundly moving. His interviews on screen motivated us to contact Camilo at the very beginning of our planning for the Truth Commission.

When we finally met him face to face in March 2010, we also discovered his gracious smile, his sense of humor, and warm, calming presence. His daughter Samantha, aged ten, accompanied him. We were touched by the deep love between them. She wore a pink dress printed with flowers and flashed a huge beautiful smile when we met her. She was remarkably poised and comfortable in a room full of adults, though she clearly had a restless curiosity and impish spirit. She liked to play tricks on her sitter, and she kept busy during the hearing by reading the books she brought, playing with stickers, and strolling around outside. She gave Gabriella one of the stickers—a star—to put on her robe.

Camilo was born in Nicaragua in 1975. He tells the story of his parents and early upbringing briefly in his war memoir, *Road from ar Ramadi: The Private Rebellion of Staff Sergeant Camilo Mejía*. The story of his parents would make for a powerful novel, one we hope to read someday. Camilo's father had studied in a Roman Catholic seminary to become a priest, but when he met the passionate and beautiful seventeen-year-old from Costa Rica who would become Camilo's mother, he had already become a well-known musician and radio personality. His father's education in liberation theology grounded his lifelong commitment to justice making, despite his abandonment of the road to priesthood. These ideas also shaped Camilo's life. Camilo's parents were prominent members of the Sandinista revolutionary movement that helped to bring down the dictatorship of Anastasio Somoza. Camilo was named for Camilo Torres, a radical priest who died fighting for justice in Colombia. His second name, Ernesto, honors Ernesto "Che" Guevara.

Camilo was raised a privileged son of revolutionaries. Camilo's mother reported directly to the top leaders in the Sandinista movement, such as Humberto Ortega. Though his parents separated shortly after his birth, his father continued to be a strong presence in his life. In Managua, Camilo attended a private Jesuit school and lived with his mother and older brother Carlos, traveling at times to visit family in New York City and Costa Rica. His father, who lived a couple of blocks away in the same neighborhood of elegant homes, had a chauffeur, whom he called "the comrade who drives for me."

When the Sandinista government lost the 1990 elections, the new government was friendly to the United States and its capitalist agenda and included former Sandinista leaders who had become multimillionaires. But because Camilo's parents had not chosen to amass wealth, his mother decided to move back to her native Costa Rica with her sons. There, Camilo was confronted with deep xenophobia toward Nicaraguan immigrants. He was taunted, shunned, and called names by his classmates. No longer one of the golden children of the revolution but an unwelcome guest, he became a lonely teenager who took consolation in reading novels and poetry and attending theaters and concerts alone.

In 1994, Camilo's grandmother, a naturalized U.S. citizen, obtained a green card for her daughter and her children. At eighteen, Camilo found himself in Miami, Florida. Even with the support money his father still sent, his mother's job as a supermarket cashier, and rental income from her Managua apartment, the family lacked enough to survive. So Camilo went to work cleaning a fast-food restaurant. His day started with work at 5:30 a.m. and ended after night school at 10 p.m. Graduation was lonely, as he had no friends to celebrate with. After receiving his diploma from the principal's office, Camilo sat on a bench outside a supermarket staring at it, puzzled about his future.

Camilo enrolled in a community college, but kept the menial fast-food job, where he had become a cook. After two years, he lost his federal student financial aid because he was supposedly making enough at his job. Disappointed, demoralized, and anxious about his future, Camilo met a U.S. Army recruiter.

The recruiter helped Camilo see the possibility of belonging to something important and of finding meaning in a land where he felt foreign, lonely, and unfulfilled. It was like a sudden revelation. Finally, he thought, he would fit in, find friends, and contribute to a larger good:

> I would say that lacking a sense of belonging at the time was the single-most important reason I joined the army. I also would argue that holds true for a lot of other people as well. The military offers a sense of family and camaraderie that's just as appealing to young people as financial stability. I also didn't feel ready for college at the time, and felt that the military would provide the "worldly experiences and maturity" I needed before getting a college education.

Camilo joined at nineteen in 1995. His surprised parents challenged his decision on political grounds. Politics aside, they also simply did not see Camilo as a soldier type who would fit in the Army. Camilo's mother warned him he would wind up in a war. She cried when he left for Fort Benning, Georgia.

PEOPLE WHO UNDERTAKE military service share the same life aspirations of many of us: they want to be part of something larger than their individual lives, to be of service to others, to do the right thing, and to have a better life. Regardless of their original reasons for entering military service, Joshua, Kevin, Tyler, Mac, Herm, Pamela, and Camilo were profoundly changed by war in their lives, for the rest of their lives. No amount of commitment, patriotic fervor, or physical and mental training can prepare a moral human being for the actual experience of war or for loving someone who returns from war. Which is what makes war, the subject of chapter 2, so devastating.

2
Killing Changes You

Nothing ever prepares you for . . . the unmeasured killing of civilians, nothing ever
prepares you for what that does to you as a
human being . . . to kill an innocent person.

CAMILO ERNESTO MEJÍA

In World War II, almost 75 percent of combat soldiers did not fire
directly at the enemy, even when their own lives were at risk. In his
landmark 1947 study, the official U.S. Army historian Brigadier General L. S. A. Marshall revealed that despite training, propaganda, and
social sanctions, soldiers retained a deep inhibition when it came to
taking human lives.

The average and normally healthy individual—the man that can
endure the mental and physical stresses of combat—still has such
an inner and usually unrealized resistance toward killing a fellow
man that he will not of his own volition take life if it is possible
to turn away from that responsibility. . . . At a vital point, he becomes a conscientious objector, unknowing.[1]

17

Marshal's statistics surprised and alarmed Army leadership. They developed new training techniques to overcome this reluctance to killing, which they called "reflexive fire training." Soldiers were conditioned to shoot before thinking. In the documentary *Soldiers of Conscience*, Major Pete Kilner describes the training: "It becomes muscle memory. You don't think about it, you just do it." Reflexive fire training raised shooting rates to 50 or 60 percent in Korea, and 85 to 90 percent in Vietnam. Kilner notes, "People are more lethal than they [the Army] ever imagined." But he also acknowledges: "The problem with reflexive fire training is that it does bypass, in some sense, [the soldiers'] moral decision-making process."

What happens after a person kills another human being? In his best seller *What It Is Like to Go to War*, Vietnam veteran Karl Marlantes claims that his Marine Corps training taught him how to kill but did not prepare him for its deeper emotional and spiritual consequences. He describes boot camp as an initiation that strips societal inhibitions against killing and transforms young men and women into killers. However, the Corps offered no preparation or guidance on what to do when conscience strikes, whether in the immediate aftermath of killing or upon returning home.

"In country," Marlantes had been fine. He felt satisfied and at times even elated by killing people he saw as "enemies." He was just doing his job as a Marine. Marlantes confesses that it took him ten years to feel any real, deep feeling about his killing in Vietnam. When he did, it shattered him. Today, Marlantes views his early reaction as a disassociation from his own humanity. He hopes that military training can include spiritual guidance that will better prepare soldiers to cope with the consequences of their actions while in combat. But can there ever be adequate preparation for the psychological and spiritual consequences of killing?

Mac

Mac still keeps many mementos of this time in the Marine Corps: pictures, manuals, a log of his rifle marksmanship. A few years ago, out of curiosity, he attended a reunion of his Officer's Basic School Class at Quantico. But in his more personal articles and scholarly papers, he often refers to his war journals, in which he chronicles the shattering of his moral universe. He notes how his understanding of war, the military, and his self-identity has changed dramatically since his childhood and military training days. Mac sees those training days as a part of his transformation: "I was leaving behind, forever, a way of life, an identity, a personality, and all that I cherished and held sacred for the past twenty-one years."[2]

At Marine Corps training in Quantico, Virginia, Mac embraced the "mythology" of the warrior. A brilliant student, he felt proud to become part of a long line of chivalrous warriors ready to sacrifice his life for God, his country, and his comrades.

Marine Corps training was truly a life-altering experience. What ultimately enables a Marine to ignore the ethical limits normally placed on the use of violence—to kill and to die in battle—is not abstract ideology, but a personal code of honor, self-respect, loyalty, and accountability to one's comrades. I learned my lessons well and readily embraced the mythology of the warrior. Upon completion of my training, I became part of a proud and chivalrous tradition, a select brotherhood of noble and courageous knights, empowered by God and country to exorcize the demonic agents of evil. I was prepared to kill and to selflessly sacrifice my life, if need be, for right and for good. After Ralphie's death and the sacrifices of the Old Ones, how could I do anything less?

Yet, as soon as Mac arrived in Vietnam, he was assigned to the 26th Marine Regimental Landing Team. Upon encountering war firsthand, he quickly realized he was ill prepared to face its actual horrors. No one was. He witnessed what he had only heard about as a child: war could be both utterly devastating and exhilarating. He saw how "killing became orgasmic, and death performance art."

For a long time, Mac shared his own war experiences, hoping that they would help people understand more deeply the tragedy of war. Today, he still speaks publicly about war and its effects, but he no longer shares his war stories. He suspects that they somehow thrill and titillate people fascinated by the pornography of violence, and he wants no part in it. But Mac still wants people to hear about the effects of combat and the death of his soul and those of his comrades.

When he speaks as a former combatant, Mac often reads from a poem he wrote while in Vietnam, "Warrior's Dance" (*Tai Chi Chuan*).

> I fear I am no longer alien to this horror.
> I am, I am, I am the horror.
> I have lost my humanity
> and have embraced the insanity of war.
> The monster and I are one.
> . . .
> The blood of innocents forever stains my soul!
> The transformation is complete,
> and I can never return.
> *Mea culpa, mea culpa, mea maxima culpa.*

Mac felt he was placed in a morally untenable situation. He was sent to war to "protect and liberate," when, in reality, he was forced to kill indiscriminately, a killing that became too easy. Deaths of the innocent became meaningless in the morass of killing. Surviving and safeguarding his comrades became his priority. He did what "had to be done":

Patriotic hymns and anthems quickly fade amidst the screams of the mutilated and the dying. As the warrior's mythology crumbled, I felt an overwhelming burden of responsibility, no longer to Corps and Country, but to those whose lives depended upon my abilities and decisions. I saw Ralphie in each of their young faces, made empty and hardened by war, and was deafened by the heart-breaking and poignant cries of parents pleading for the lives of their children. Survival was all that really mattered. What I failed to realize at the time, however, was that, at least in spirit, we were all dead already.

Mac also saw some men who actually embraced war and who were exhilarated by the godlike power it gave them. Intoxicated by war, they hated to see it end because they could no longer function outside its frenzy. He heard some men say that killing "meant nothing." Yet, Mac also knew that most soldiers did not go to war to get high on killing and to murder innocent people.

Most exert great effort, often at considerable personal risk, to protect the innocent and conduct themselves with decency and integrity. Unfortunately, either under the rubric of "supreme emergency," as was the case in World War II, or due to the morally untenable conditions of guerrilla/counterinsurgency warfare, as in Vietnam and Iraq, soldiers inevitably are positioned to become the unwitting instruments of slaughter. Such occurrences are always tragic and regrettable, but never more so than when war is misguided and unnecessary. . . . We are the victims of politicians' hypocrisy, the scapegoats for the inevitable affront to the national conscience, and the sacrificial lambs sent to slaughter in retribution for our collective guilt and inadequacies. In fact, no one knows the sacrilege of war better than we who must fight it and then have to live with the memories of what we have done and what we have become.

Mac later came to admire the people with the courage to become conscientious objectors and to say, "War no more." Today, he regrets not just walking away and attributes his continuing to fight to a lack of courage. Coming home brought him no closure or relief. Instead, returning home was the beginning of an ever-deepening reckoning with what he had done and who he had become.

Herm

As a draftee, Herm went through basic training, which taught him combat skills, including hand-to-hand combat and killing. He still remembers the shock of having to shout, "Kill! Kill! Kill! Kill without mercy!" After Advanced Individual Training at Fort Dix, Herm was sent to Fort Belvoir as a chaplain's assistant. As a combat-prepared soldier, he was responsible for the safety of his ministry team, because chaplains do not receive combat training and do not carry weapons. Herm faced this responsibility during an extremely tense time for the military. His supervisor was first in line to be Senior Chaplain if the United States invaded Cuba, a threat so imminent that the Pentagon held planning sessions and briefings. The military services had to coordinate their chaplains for the invasion. Herm describes this period of frantic preparation as "exciting, but frightening at the same time." It was also a time that would set the course of his entire adult career:

> The chaplains assigned there at Fort Belvoir were well-educated and experienced chaplains who impressed me as mentors. Since I had three years of college under my belt, they asked me to run the youth group and protected my back when I had to make some difficult choices. . . . It went so well that the chaplains encouraged me to come back as a military chaplain.

Herm took their advice. He left his military duties to complete college and seminary at Calvin Theological Seminary. During his graduate studies, he studied the ethical principles of the Christian just-war tradition, which dates back to the fifth century. His professor taught him to look at the reasons the government stated for going to war and the strategy and tactics for the conduct of the war. Herm concluded that the United States was conducting an unjust war in Vietnam, especially because the intended outcome would be a divided country and stalemate like Korea.

I wondered if I wanted to put myself at risk going into military chaplaincy with that assessment of the war. My seminary mentors felt that I was exactly the right person at the right time. They knew that many fighting the war did not believe in it, but they were trapped because they were not pacifists who could be conscientious objectors. These soldiers would need a champion to help them object on principles of just war. They turned out to be correct—many moral men were trapped. One of my greatest moral agonies of Vietnam is the refusal of our military to honor the conscientious objection of those who were not against all war but were against the Vietnam War.

Herm was ordained in the Christian Reformed Church in 1968 and became a U.S. Army captain and chaplain. The military put him through the Chaplain Basic Course, which focused on the history and function of the chaplaincy, on writing military correspondence, on how to wear the uniform correctly, and on passing the physical fitness test. His first few months, he was assigned to a basic training unit, where he joined the troops for their training. He crawled through the infiltration course, went to the shooting ranges, took the fitness test as often as three times a week, and never missed being on the range for hand-to-hand combat. On the ranges, troops shouted, "Kill! Kill! Kill!" the loudest and most intensely. The range was also where the reality of combat became most real. Herm found he had to do extensive counseling with many weeping soldiers who were distraught by what they were required to do.

Because he was older than many of his peers, Herm knew he would be sent to Vietnam, and he was. He began his tour six months later. In country, Herm was first assigned to the 1st Infantry Division just north of Saigon on the base at Lai Kai. His chapel was located on a former Michelin rubber plantation. However, he worked offsite much of the time because he wanted to be with the soldiers in combat. He wanted to be there for them as they returned after weeks in the jungle. Herm struggled with how to address the moral struggles of those he served.

I was on Thunder Road the second week in Nam. Track vehicles and tanks were evenly spaced along the route for security. I stopped at the first armored personnel carrier, talked a bit and asked when they last had Communion or Mass. Most had never had it in-country. One soldier told me that he felt chaplains had forgotten that wherever two or three are gathered there was a worshipping community. So we had Communion.

Herm read to the soldiers from a Protestant communion liturgy, which concludes with these words of forgiveness and love:

That we may be nourished with Christ, the true bread from heaven, let us lift up our hearts to Christ Jesus, our advocate, at the right hand of his heavenly Father. . . .

Take, eat, remember, and believe that the body of our Lord Jesus Christ was given for the complete forgiveness of all our sins. . . . Take, drink, remember, and believe that the precious blood of our Lord Jesus Christ was shed for the complete forgiveness of all our sins.

Beloved in the Lord, since the Lord has now nourished our souls at his table, let us jointly praise his holy name with thanksgiving. . . . Psalm 103:

Praise the Lord, O my soul;
. . . The Lord is compassionate and
gracious, slow to anger, abounding in love.
He does not treat us as our sins deserve or
repay us according to our iniquities . . .

In this simple ritual with its ancient plea for mercy and deliverance, Herm discovered a key to his career as a chaplain in war.

It was a wonderful experience for those four young men and me. I could feel the ritual grounding them. After we finished, my Jeep headed down the road. The soldiers who had just received Communion called down to the entire row of security vehicles, and every one of them stopped me to have Communion. I could hear the radio broadcasting from the tanks to the headquarters. It crackled with voices rejoicing that they had Communion. A deep moral hunger and thirst was quenched in this meal together. The eloquence of the Sacrament brought healing.

Herm's initial decision to serve Communion to the troops influenced his entire career. He offered it at every service he conducted thereafter, even in the fields where soldiers were training for war. "Wounded soldiers who knew me asked for Communion as they waited in Triage. I felt that God was healing something in them through me, some deep moral pain."

Herm spent as much time, or more, in the combat zone as other members of his unit, and he saw three things that shook him to the core. He saw soldiers mutilating enemy bodies, such as cutting off ears as souvenirs. He also had to report a mass killing of captured Vietnamese people. But the third thing troubled him the most: the behavior of the senior enlisted leaders (NCOs) and the officer corps.

Their standard practice was six months in combat, then six months in a rear job. I saw young NCOs fight the battles all through their tour, while senior NCOs never put themselves in harm's way. A battalion or brigade commander would get his ticket punched, and, just when he had gained some proficiency in combat leadership, he was replaced by someone inexperienced and usually less competent. The resulting loss of life was unconscionable.

Herm's objection to the last crisis, especially, was a problem when the 1st Infantry Division began returning to the United States. In a leadership pattern he opposed on moral grounds, he was assigned to a rear position. As Herm struggled with this safer assignment, he received a call from Chaplain (LTC) Kelly, in charge of the 4th Division, who told Herm that he had an outstanding reputation as a troop chaplain. Kelly had a unit that had just gone through a major command crisis, and they needed an experienced chaplain. At Kelly's invitation, Herm headed north to the Central Highland, grateful for his new assignment. When he arrived there, Herm, who was a tad over 5'9" tall and weighed 105 pounds, needed to rest. However, after three days, he became restless, so he joined an infantry unit called the "Regulars By God."

Herm personally experienced and witnessed in others the crisis of conscience that led soldiers, whether volunteers or conscripts, to solidify their commitments not to fight in an immoral war. Yet, they had to serve. The cost to their moral consciences was tremendous.

I noticed that my experience was different from those who were combatants, especially those who had taken life or watched innocent people be maimed or killed. I was amazed at their personal shame—not guilt—but profound, searing shame. Many felt that they had committed a personal affront against God. My religious training helped me see that what they were confronting is what many experience as sin, and I tried to minister to their broken souls.

Awareness of their shame and sin emerged, especially when I gave them the Imprecatory Psalms to read. Their reactions both amazed and amused me. I could sense them being caught up in the poet's mood and tone.

Psalm 51 is traditionally identified as a prayer of David, and it is one Herm used often. As David's plea for cleansing, it reflects, perhaps, the story in II Samuel 11–12. In these chapters, King David took notice of Bathsheba, the wife of one of his best generals, and coerced her into a sexual relationship. He then arranged for her husband's death in order to cover up her pregnancy. The prophet Nathan, who detected the crime, skillfully elicited from the king an admission of shame and remorse, a story told in II Samuel 12. Psalm 51 reflects David's contrition:

Have mercy upon me, O God, according to thy loving kindness:
according unto the multitude of thy tender mercies blot out my
transgressions.

Wash me thoroughly from mine iniquity, and cleanse me from
my sin.

For I acknowledge my transgressions: and my sin is ever before
me . . .

Hide thy face from my sins, and blot out all mine iniquities.

Create in me a clean heart, O God; and renew a right spirit within
me.

Cast me not away from thy presence; and take not thy holy spirit
from me.

Restore unto me the joy of thy salvation; and uphold me with thy
free spirit.

Then will I teach transgressors thy ways; and sinners shall be con-
verted unto thee.

Deliver me from bloodguiltiness, O God, thou God of my salvation:
and my tongue shall sing aloud of thy righteousness. . . .

The sacrifices of God are a broken spirit: a broken and a contrite
heart, O God, thou wilt not despise. (KJV)

Herm observed that, when soldiers finished reading, they would
look at him and the Bible quizzically and ask if he had a special chaplain's Bible or if the Psalm was in any Bible. This opened a door for
Herm to ask about their feelings about the war: "How did it feel for
you to read Psalm 51? How did it feel to be both Nathan and David at
the same time?" They would often describe their feelings of betrayal
by their government but also their own shame and guilt. From these
conversations, Herm concluded that something profound and soul en-
dangering was the source of their suffering, not just "shell shock," or
what was later called PTSD.

Despite knowing he provided valuable support for soldiers fighting
in Vietnam, Herm continued to struggle with his work and the war's
mission. When the North Vietnamese Army attacked his unit in the

middle of the night while they slept, Herm was injured by shrapnel and received a concussion and fractured skull. When Herm refused hospitalization in order to help with the other wounded, the more severely injured soldier next to him offered him his flak jacket for protection. Herm dragged several soldiers to the battalion surgeon's bunker and also treated some himself. One soldier he treated lost the back of his head to one of the mortars; Herm gave him a tracheotomy and an IV to clot his blood and keep him hydrated. That difficult night of intense suffering for so many increased Herm's moral objections to the war in Vietnam.

Herm's second injury ended his tour. He was riding in a helicopter when the pilot turned to avoid high-tension wires, but he hit them with the tail rotor, which snapped off. The main top blades threw the copter into an erratic flight pattern, and Herm was suddenly ejected. He fell into tall elephant grass and tumbled about two hundred feet. Both his arms were nearly shattered. Only when the pilot came to visit him at the evacuation hospital did Herm realize what he had survived. The pilot noted that the altimeter was at a hundred seventy-five feet when Herm left the copter, in what should have been a fatal fall.

Pamela

Pamela's son, Dweylon, enlisted on March 7, 2001, just after his seventeenth birthday, and completed his basic and advanced training with great success. Then, the events of September 11 unfolded, and Pamela knew everything had changed. She began to worry and called everyone she knew in military service to see how to get her son out of the Army. She considered conscientious objector status, but she didn't think he was prepared to apply. The military was like his family. Eventually, she realized he had no real options. When he was sent on an overseas assignment to Kuwait, she knew he would almost certainly be sent into a war in the region.

Pamela's son, her youngest child, was deployed in the 2003 "Shock and Awe" invasion of Iraq and was among the first U.S. troops to enter the country. As his unit drove through Kuwait and into Iraq, he remembers seeing the terrible living conditions of the people and his shock that people could survive them. At barely nineteen years of age, he did not understand the situation he was in, though "it felt wrong as soon as we were there; I knew that, but I couldn't put my finger on why." He was helped by his superior officer. When he arrived in Iraq, this senior NCO told him point blank that the war they would fight was not just: "we were not there for the right reasons but for money." The officer explained that he didn't want to deceive them with ideas and information that he thought were inaccurate or untrue because he owed them the truth, and he wanted them to fight with their eyes open. They would see battle and had to fight, but when they returned to the United States and were free of the situation, they would have a better understanding of why this war was wrong.

Dweylon served in Iraq for eight months in the rear behind a Patriot missile unit. And he did his duties as best he could in order to keep his comrades safe. He gathered intelligence about the geography of the region and troop movements, repaired vehicles, and maintained weapons for his fellow soldiers. In his role of organizing communications, he delivered orders to officers who vastly outranked him and provided crucial information to commanders on the frontlines. Not wanting to be a weak link in his unit, he worked sixteen-hour days and did his very best to help his unit stay safe. He believes that, though he never had to fire a weapon and kill someone, he is as morally culpable in killing innocent people as those who did. His efforts helped his comrades do their job better and stay alive. He also knows that he does not understand the personal cost of actual killing, but accepts that his role in an immoral war was the same as those who did the killing. He finds it difficult to talk about what he did. Until Dweylon and his mother participated in an interview together for this book, she did not know much about his experience in Iraq, beyond being in the rear guard following a Patriot missile unit. Though she had tried to get him to talk, he was always reticent.

Pamela knew her son remained in a rear detachment, but she also knew that the nature of the war often blurred the lines of battle. Her own military training and weapons procurement work had taught her about the dangers of fighting an insurgency, and she understood the very real threats her son faced every day. She regretted agreeing to let her baby enlist at such a young, vulnerable age.

At the seminary where Pamela studied for her doctorate, sentiment against the war was passionate. While Pamela agreed with that sentiment, she found the simple moral judgments and prejudice against the military devastating. The atmosphere at the seminary was enlivening for war protestors but lacked serious conversation about the risks to military personnel.

> During one of my classes, it got to me. I said, "Listen, my son is over there. I want us to have peace, but I can't tolerate your talking about soldiers like this. One of these soldiers is my son." I left class that day before it was over.

Pamela wrote her dissertation on theories of just war in Pan-African traditions, while she endured the constant anguish of not knowing whether her beloved son was dead or alive. Once, at a meeting of mentors and scholarship recipients of the United Methodist Women of Color Scholars Program, she presented a section of her dissertation material. At the end of her presentation, she paused to gather herself and then in just seven words that held all the weight she was carrying, she said, "My son is in Iraq right now." The women, who respected her as a scholar and minister, also could understand Pamela's anguish as a mother, and they prayed together for her and her son.

During the entire time Dweylon served in Iraq, Pamela received only five succinct letters from him, saying he was OK and thanking her for things she'd sent, especially wet wipes, soap, and candy. His phone calls happened less than once a month, and his letters were agonizingly slow to arrive. Once, she had put together another care package for Dweylon and had taken it to the post office. She asked the clerk why his letters were taking such a very long time to reach her.

The woman at the window scolded me: "Well ma'am, you have to understand, we're in a war." I went ballistic. I started weeping like a baby and said, "You don't have to tell me we're in a war! My son is over there. Look at the address on this box I'm giving you." I walked out, and I never went back to that location, ever again. I had a mental breakdown in that post office, it hurt me so bad.

For many months, Pamela was unable to bring herself to tell her daughter about Dweylon. Her daughter lived in Georgia and was the intense worrier in the family. She had always been extremely sensitive and close to her brother. Pamela notes, "I did not have it in me" to tell her daughter about Dweylon and take care of her emotional needs while also pastoring a church, surviving her doctoral work, and worrying about her son. So she let her daughter think her brother was in Kuwait. Isolated by her anguishing secret, she left the television on at home all the time, constantly reviewing the faces of U.S. military casualties. She lived in dissociated pieces, an exhausted wreck. When her daughter called, she began to realize her mother played the television constantly, and she worried about her mother's obsessive watching of the news. She tried to reassure Pamela by telling her Dweylon was safe in Kuwait, and she pressured her mother to stop watching TV. Pamela did not tell her daughter where her brother was until he was coming home.

Camilo

Camilo excelled in his three years of active military duty, which he spent mostly in Fort Hood, Texas, in the 4th Infantry Division. He enjoyed the discipline and the physical challenges and always received good performance reviews. He was known for speaking his mind on a few occasions, but without getting into any serious trouble.

When he was ready to go home after his third year of active service, he discovered that the military recruiter had misrepresented the terms of his service. At Fort Hood, another recruiter explained to Camilo that his commitment was really for eight years, as it was for all who entered military service. Therefore, Camilo owed the Army five more years. He had three options for fulfilling his contract: he could stay in the regular army; he could sign up for the Inactive Ready Reserve (IRR); or he could join the National Guard. Regardless of his choice, he learned he could always be called back into active duty for the remaining five years of his contract—a "detail" that most recruiters spend little or no time explaining or that they reassuringly dismiss as a very remote and unlikely possibility. Camilo decided to join the Florida National Guard; he was assured that, as a guardsman, he would most likely only be called back to active duty for relief operations after natural disasters.

Camilo went back to college. After two years at Miami Dade Community College, he transferred to the University of Miami, only to discover that the National Guard would not cover tuition for a private school. Camilo covered the tuition himself, half with a merit scholarship and half with a student loan. Despite his financial struggles, Camilo thrived in college. He majored in psychology, was a member of several honor societies, and prepared to apply to a doctoral program. He also did volunteer work for his community as a crisis counselor, supported people living with HIV/AIDS, and worked with homeless communities in his area. His daughter Samantha was born during this period.

As 2003 started, Camilo was looking forward to the month of May, when he would graduate and finish his eight-year commitment to the military. But on January 14, the Florida National Guard was summoned to participate in Operation Iraqi Freedom. Not only did Camilo have to go to war but also because of a "stop-loss order," Camilo's contract with the military was extended to 2031. Ten weeks later, he left for the Middle East.

When Camilo joined the military, he thought that the United States would go to war only for a very good cause: "to bring freedom to other lands." Even during the lead-up to the war in Iraq, he opposed it for political reasons: he did not believe there was evidence Iraq had weapons of mass destruction, and he was convinced a war would be illegal and driven by economic interests. Yet, he did not speak out publicly against it. He did not want to be seen as a coward or to tarnish his excellent military record. As an infantry squad leader, he felt responsible for his men; they needed him, he thought. He was torn, but when he was deployed to the Middle East, he thought he could put his principles aside, do his duty, and hang on to go back home to his daughter.

Their first stop was the border between Jordan and Iraq. Officially, the United States was not at war with Iraq. Most soldiers in Camilo's platoon, however, could not wait to put their training to the test and enter combat. Camilo overheard someone singing, "Give War a Chance." Thinking about his daughter and the heritage he wanted to leave her, Camilo risked a simple, symbolic gesture. He surreptitiously wrote "GIVE PEACE A CHANCE" on a piece of paper. That night, while he shared night duty with a squad member he trusted, Camilo asked him to take a picture of him carrying the sign in his hands in his full military gear. Camilo then immediately threw the sign away, but the picture remains today as a telltale witness to his objection to the war.

When the "shock and awe" bombing of Baghdad began, Camilo was appalled that the United States violated international law. Without prior notice, his entire company was awakened at 3 a.m. and ordered to get ready to go. Soldiers, confused by the sudden orders, were mistakenly overjoyed, thinking they were going home, an indication, perhaps, of the evaporation of their desire to see combat once reality hit. Then, they realized what was really happening: they were going to Iraq. At that moment, Camilo understood that he was utterly unprepared for the reality of war:

Nothing ever prepares you for going to Iraq and seeing the destruction of an entire nation. Nothing ever prepares you for . . . the unmeasured killing of civilians, nothing ever prepares you for what that does to you as a human being . . . to kill an innocent person. Nothing is going to really prepare you for the level of destruction that you bring upon a nation and you bring upon yourself for being a part of it. And yet I have a conscience, you know, which goes way beyond any law, it goes way beyond any order that I can receive.[3]

At one point in his tour, Camilo's squad faced a crowd of protesters. Taking shelter in a building, Camilo held a position on the roof with others in his squad. He had his gun sights on an adolescent young man who appeared to have a grenade in his hand. Camilo was ordered to shoot. He had no awareness of firing, but when he took shelter in a closet by himself and examined his gun magazine, he counted eleven bullets missing. He still has no memory of shooting. All he remembers is the young man standing and then lying dead in a pool of blood in the dirt. He was appalled that his ability to decide what to do had been taken away by his training.

Camilo observed ongoing, systematic abuses of prisoners of war, often innocent civilians or petty criminals arrested randomly in the streets, abuses depicted in the 2007 Academy Award–winning documentary *Taxi to the Dark Side* by Alex Gibney. In the Al Asad prisoner-of-war camp, Camilo saw troops constantly yelling and ordering so-called "enemy combatants" to stand up and sit down to deprive them of sleep for forty-eight hours. He witnessed prisoners being blindfolded with black hoods, their hands tied behind them while their genitalia were "inspected" for no reason, or they endured mock executions when a soldier simulated the sound of bombings with a gun or a sledgehammer. One day, Camilo's battalion was put in charge of the torture of the prisoners. While he took pride in always participating in anything he ordered his soldiers to do, Camilo used his rank that day to watch, rather than conduct, the abuse of the prisoners. He completely opposed the inhumane treatment of the detainees, but he was afraid to speak out. When the Abu Ghraib scandal erupted much later, Camilo knew that it was not about a few "bad apples"; the practice of torture was pervasive and came from way up the chain of command.

In country, Camilo increasingly distrusted his commanders. He realized that they were more concerned about advancing their careers and receiving medals than protecting their men or avoiding the senseless killing and maiming of innocent civilians. His feelings were common, and, for Camilo, they led to a deep sense of betrayal.

When his Florida National Guard Unit was sent to the city of ar Ramadi, Camilo experienced the full force of the Iraqis' resistance to the U.S. occupation. His unit was ambushed and bombed, and they felt constantly threatened. His remaining combat-thirsty comrades had a change of attitude: most just wanted to get out of Iraq alive. They hoped people in the United States would do as much as possible to bring the troops home. Camilo commented:

> Perhaps because of my constant proximity to death and after los-ing hope someone at home would get us out of the war, I started commending my body and soul to God every day. . . . Before go-ing to sleep, I would always say a little prayer. At first it was a simple request for God to let me see my daughter, Samantha, one more time. As time went by, I widened my prayers to ask for the safety and well-being of all the soldiers in my unit, and then started praying for all the soldiers in Iraq and their families. Before long I was praying for the families of the Iraqis we killed during our missions. And then one day I realized I was even praying for our enemies, and for an end to violence in Iraq, and then for an end to all war.[4]

One day, Camilo joined some other soldiers and participated in a chaplain's ritual of baptism. He was immersed in the waters of the biblical Euphrates. He was twenty-seven and his feeling of being close to God made him feel more deeply connected to all human beings. Yet, this compassion for humanity did not hinder his ability to shoot when his life and the lives of those around him were threatened. He confesses that he went "into a trance in which the only thing that mattered was survival and everything else was erased from my conscience."[5]

While in country, Camilo's green card was about to expire. Ac-cording to military regulation, eight years was the maximum extent of time a non-U.S. citizen could legally be part of the U.S. Army. Camilo was nearing the end of his eighth year when he was deployed to Iraq, so his time was running out while he was in country. He wrote a letter to his captain requesting to be sent home to take care of this limit. After a long and complicated battle with his superiors and the bureaucracy of the Army, Camilo was finally granted a two-week leave to attend to his visa issues. Though he felt guilty leaving his unit behind, he also could not wait to leave a war he thought was wrong. He was hoping that stateside, he would be legally prohibited from returning to Iraq, but he found out that he was expected to return.

JOSHUA CASTEEL WAS assigned to the army's 202nd Military Intelligence Battalion as an Arabic translator and U.S. Army interrogator inside the prison at Abu Ghraib, where he was to be part of the "cleanup crew" following the prisoner abuse scandal. He was disturbed to find that the prisoners were being referred to as "detainees," which stripped them of their rights under the Geneva Conventions. It made him want a promotion and greater authority to protect prisoners. At the same time, he wondered "what . . . a blond, blue-eyed Iowan boy is doing in Iraq in the first place . . . at least with Caesar's body armor and an M-16."[6]

After five months at Abu Ghraib, Joshua had done over a hundred interrogations. He concluded that 95 percent of the men he interrogated were neither terrorists nor insurgents; they were just ordinary taxi drivers, fathers, imams, and farmers. One fourteen-year-old boy was terrified because he would miss his school exams. Finally, however, Joshua got a thick file that showed he was facing a real enemy who needed serious grilling, a Saudi man who had purposefully crossed into Iraq to fight with insurgents. The man had already offered a great deal of information voluntarily. When the young man entered the room, Joshua felt annoyed that the man was polite, confident, and calm. Joshua pressured him to cause stress and assert the power of his authority over him, but was unable to unsettle him. When Joshua switched gears to ask the prisoner why he had come to kill, the man said his faith required him to defend Muslim lands invaded by non-

Muslim armies. He admitted his duty in Iraq was jihad, and if the opportunity arose, he would kill Joshua, even though he'd never fired a gun before in his life.

The man abruptly turned the tables and asked Joshua the same question. Joshua, who had not had to fire his gun at anyone, denied he entered Iraq to kill and asserted that his duty was to serve his country and to defend Iraq's people. The man rejected this answer and insisted, "If the U.S. military didn't want people to get killed, they would have sent others, not soldiers who are sent when people need to be killed." Finally, the man asked Joshua how he could call himself a Christian— Jesus had asked his followers to turn the other cheek, to pray for those who persecute you, and to love your enemies. Joshua found it strange to receive a lesson on the Sermon on the Mount from a jihadist. He began to realize they were both religious men with a strong sense of duty, devoted to their people and their religious ideals, and willing to sacrifice themselves for their beliefs. But Joshua was unsettled by the conversation. He admitted to the man that something was wrong, that in a different world, they might respect each other and not need to kill each other. Then, Joshua left the room.

> I went to my chain of command and said, "I've lost my objectivity. . . . If I go back into that room, I'm going to be seeing a twenty-two-year-old man who is looking for answers." And I didn't say this, but it is essentially what I meant: I am a twenty-four-year-old kid looking for answers and I don't care to exploit him of his information. I want to talk to him man to man about the things that matter to him and to me.[7]

This one interrogation with an enemy combatant crystallized Joshua's understanding that to follow Jesus, he had to take off the uniform. When he was sent home, he applied for and received CO status.

KEVIN BENDERMAN REALIZED at last his desire to experience war. He was deployed to Iraq in March 2003, at the war's beginning. Unlike the younger men in his unit, who, according to Kevin, viewed combat "like it was a video game they played back in their childhood," he had been a soldier for a decade, and he had just married his wife, Monica, and become a stepfather before he was deployed. He was deeply troubled by what he witnessed in Iraq. When some children threw rocks at their unit, the senior officer ordered the men to shoot at them and gun them down. He saw bombed-out homes and home-less Iraqis who lived in mud huts and drank water from dirty puddles. In one incident that haunts him, he saw a screaming young girl whose arm was black with third-degree burns and whose mother begged the soldiers for medical help as their convoy passed by. Kevin implored an officer to stop and help her. Citing limited medical supplies as a rea-son, the officer refused her aid. Kevin later reflected on his feelings: "I had to look at that little girl, look into her eyes, and in her eyes I saw the TRUTH. I cannot kill."

Near the Iranian border in Khanagin, Kevin saw mass graves where dogs fed off the dead bodies of women, men, and children. After seeing the civilian corpses, Kevin made a point of befriending ordi-nary Iraqis. But officers warned him not to fraternize with "the en-emy." Despite the warning, he had long talks with an English-speaking schoolteacher and began reading the Quran. He increasingly realized that the religious and moral values of most Iraqis were similar to his. When Kevin wrote home to his wife, Monica, he spoke of discover-ing from a man who was a part-time preacher that he was in an area of Iraq that was supposed to be the location of the biblical Garden of Eden. Why, he wrote, was he "walking around the Garden of Eden with a gun?"[8]

When he came home in September 2003, Kevin began to rethink everything he had thought about war.

> I have learned from firsthand experience that war is the destroyer of everything that is good in the world; it turns our young into soulless killers, and we tell them that they are heroes when they master the "art" of killing. That is a very deranged mindset in my opinion. It destroys the environment, life, and the resources that could be used to create more life by advancing our endeavors.[9]

In late 2004, Kevin, through a stop-loss order, was told to return to Iraq, and he realized he could not go back. After extensive discussions with Monica about what he should do, he realized he had come to believe war was wrong, all wars.

TYLER BOUDREAU WENT to marine boot camp in 1989, when no armed conflicts involving the United States were on the horizon. Despite the absence of war talk, Tyler went through his training, knowing that battle was indeed part of what he wanted to experience. In fact, he craved war, but by the time it arrived, he had been in so long, he had a choice to retire or go to Iraq. He went, despite his doubts about the purpose of the war in Iraq, the prospects for meeting its goals, and the impact on the Iraqi people.

Primary among Tyler's assignments was dispatching units around an area of operations and tracking Iraqi activities. From the moment he was in country, Tyler found himself utterly humbled by the humanity of the Iraqi people. This sensibility challenged and greatly inhibited him. Tyler was bewildered by the audacity of officers who imposed their will on the people and the capacity of some of his peers to order artillery and air attacks, commandeer buildings and roads, and abuse prisoners. However, Tyler did his job, and sometimes, he did it with enthusiasm.

One such operation was "Operation Trash Lutifiyah," in northern Babil province, just south of Baghdad, where U.S. troops had taken heavy casualties. The strategic operation also served to meet a desire for vengeance. All buildings, apartments, stores, rooms—even closets—were to be systematically trashed. People's belonging were tossed into the streets. The houses of possible insurgents received a particularly vigorous trashing. Iraqi males of military age were already in detention, making the women and children the only eyewitnesses to the systematic destruction of everything they had. That night, Tyler instructed his men to go back to the houses of the suspected "bad guys" and trash them yet again. The point was to send a clear message. And those women and children, retraumatized in the middle of the night, would have certainly relayed the message to their men.

We still know where you live, motherfucker. And we are not going away. . . . Every night for the next two weeks, I directed another few homes to be trashed, and every night, as Marines carried out those orders, the emergency grew a little stronger. We called it *Operation Trash Lutifiyah*, but I think a more apt title would have been *Operation Trash all rapport with the Iraqi people*."[10]

While Tyler takes responsibility for actions that he now regrets, he also understands them as military orders he had to fulfill. He can also see now how the years of training in the Marines desensitized him to killing and dulled his natural ability to think critically. He was trained to kill. He was trained to hate the "bad guys" and not to ask many questions about what made them "bad."

At odds with his conscience, Tyler started to withdraw from the military environment and ideology, seeking to know, again, his own capacity for moral judgment. He took up smoking for the first time in his life and tried to spend as much time as possible by himself when off duty. The need to belong was not as strong as the need to understand who he was, what he was doing, and who he wanted to be.

After witnessing, ordering, or engaging in war's atrocities, many soldiers acknowledge something deep changes in them. The shift can take place right away, or it can take many years or even decades to be realized. Most soldiers do not feel prepared for how war changes them. And when they come back from war, they find it hard to articulate and discuss.

Some never make it home. In 2004, Colonel Theodore Westhusing, a professor of English and philosophy at West Point, felt compelled to volunteer to serve in Iraq because he believed that the war was just. His doctoral dissertation had focused on the virtues and ethical values of U.S. combat, and he expected that a firsthand experience of war would make him a better professor. In his early forties, he was a Roman Catholic with a wife and three children who went to Mass almost every week. Westhusing was given the title of "Director, Counter-Terrorism/Special Operations, Civilian Police Assistance Training Team, Multi-National Security Transition Command-Iraq." In March 2005, his superior officer, General David Petraeus, praised his exceptional work with Iraqi leaders and U.S. contractors. However, within months after he was commended, Westhusing, pursuing an anonymous tip, uncovered massive illegalities: gross mismanagement of resources by the contractors, forged military documents, equipment theft, improperly trained people, and abuse of the Iraqis. He was pressured to deny these findings and he complied.

In June 2005, within seven days of complying, Westhusing died of "self-inflicted wounds to the head," a month before the end of his tour of duty. At the time, he was the highest-ranking officer to die violently in Iraq. He left a farewell note written in all capital letters to General Petraeus. Westhusing's wife, Michelle, verified her husband's handwriting and noted that the letter's content matched, almost word for word, their final phone conversations. She said: "I think Ted gave his life to let everyone know what was going on."

THANKS FOR TELLING ME IT WAS A GOOD DAY UNTIL I BRIEFED YOU. [REDACTED NAME]—YOU ARE ONLY INTERESTED IN YOUR CAREER AND PROVIDE NO SUPPORT TO YOUR STAFF—NO MSN [MISSION] SUPPORT AND YOU DON'T CARE. I CANNOT SUPPORT A MSN THAT LEADS TO CORRUPTION, HUMAN RIGHTS ABUSES AND LIARS. I AM SULLIED—NO MORE. I DIDN'T VOLUNTEER TO SUPPORT CORRUPT, MONEY GRUBBING CONTRACTORS, NOR WORK FOR COMMANDERS ONLY INTERESTED IN THEMSELVES. I CAME TO SERVE HONORABLY AND FEEL DISHONORED. I TRUST NO IRAQI. I CANNOT LIVE THIS WAY. ALL MY LOVE TO MY FAMILY, MY WIFE AND MY PRECIOUS CHIL-DREN. I LOVE YOU AND TRUST YOU ONLY. DEATH BEFORE BEING DIS-HONORED ANY MORE. TRUST IS ESSENTIAL—I DON'T KNOW WHO TRUST ANYMORE [SIC]. WHY SERVE WHEN YOU CANNOT ACCOM-PLISH THE MISSION, WHEN YOU NO LONGER BELIEVE IN THE CAUSE, WHEN YOUR EVERY EFFORT AND BREATH TO SUCCEED MEETS WITH LIES, LACK OF SUPPORT, AND SELFISHNESS? NO MORE. REEVALUATE

YOURSELVES, CDRS [COMMANDERS]. YOU ARE NOT WHAT YOU THINK
YOU ARE AND I KNOW IT.
    —COL TED WESTHUSING
LIFE NEEDS TRUST. TRUST IS NO MORE FOR ME HERE IN IRAQ.[11]

SOME SOLDIERS AFTER killing or witnessing an atrocity go through
such a severe crisis of conscience that they make the very difficult
decision to refuse to return to combat. A few apply for conscientious
objector status, which is an arduous bureaucratic process that requires
an applicant to prove a change in his or her moral understanding of
"war in any form." This change, called a "crystallization of conscience," is, in effect, to have become a pacifist. Often, applicants for
CO status encounter resistance, discouragement, and challenges to
their character from their superior officers and chaplains. Other soldiers go AWOL, are court-martialed, go to jail, and are dishonorably
discharged. Still others escape to Canada or Mexico. Many decide to
stay in the military and take their chances, despite the stop-loss policy
of multiple redeployments.

    Those who survive this process and return "home" are expected to
switch almost seamlessly from a combat zone to life back home, to shift
from the urgencies and traumas of war to ordinary civilian life. They
step onto a plane or ship transport from war, receive an exit interview,
spend a few hours or days in transit, and step into the waiting arms of
their families.

    There is a boot camp to prepare for war, but there is no boot camp
to reintegrate veterans to civilian life. They were taught reflexive fire
shooting, but not how to recover a shredded moral identity.

    Often veterans feel that even the best-intentioned civilians do not
know how to welcome them home. Some celebrate them as heroes,
which thwarts veterans' needs to confess the moral ambiguities or
sense of shame about their experiences. Some act as if they hope veterans will not bring up "unpleasant" conversations in "inappropriate"
settings. Some ask mindlessly, "Did you kill someone over there?" as
if this were not part of the nature of war. Some expect veterans to

just go back to things as they were, as if nothing had happened. Some veterans notice that for a good portion of the population, the Iraq and Afghanistan wars barely even registered in their consciousness. Many veterans feel misunderstood and demonized by antiwar activists and pacifists who label them as unethical killing machines with no moral conscience.

One of the greatest challenges for many young veterans returning from Iraq and Afghanistan is to convey how these conflicts radically differ from images people have of past wars. The word "war" itself contributes to public misunderstandings of what young veterans are facing. The Afghanistan and Iraq campaigns are not wars between two countries with armies. In fact, the Army calls them "counter-insurgency operations." In such conflicts, the traditional boundaries between enemy combatants and civilians are almost completely blurred, and there are no frontlines or safe rears. U.S. troops now fight against an enemy that could be anyone and anywhere. Even a child or a pregnant woman can present a lethal danger, hiding a bomb or a grenade. No one is safe, but killing a civilian violates the code of conduct for war.

How do you go home after all of this?

3

Coming Home Is Hell

A lot of things really make sense when you're
doing them over there. But when you come back,
it's just like, "How did I do that?" It's just like a
totally different world. Everything is kind of
muted, and I'm never really happy. I don't really
enjoy things. I just feel hopeless and listless. And
I just feel like I don't fit in with other kids my age.
It's just like . . . I don't know. It's just really hard
to relate to anyone. I want, more than anybody
else, to find a meaning to my experience over
there, and something good to feel about. But I
just can't find it.

SPECIALIST JOSH MIDDLETON,
Iraq veteran[1]

Clay Warren Hunt, whose story began this book, was widely admired
for his successful return home from combat. An inspiring idealist, he
worked in disaster relief with Team Rubicon (TR), which he founded
with fellow veterans, including his friend Jake Wood. His hope for a
new life after war is touching.

45

Since separating from the Marines in May of 2009, I have been having quite a hard time re-entering civilian society. I have sorely missed the friendships and sense of purpose that I had while I served. I honestly didn't think I would ever find that anywhere else—and then Team Rubicon was born. While serving with TR in Haiti and Chile, I was able to use the skills I had learned in the Corps and I found myself alongside a band of brothers once again, who were all working towards a common goal—to help people who were in dire need of our assistance. That experience has given me a renewed sense of purpose, but more importantly, hope—a hope that I might find a place in the world where I am needed again, and that I can use the skills and the knowledge I gained by serving in the Corps to help make the world a better, brighter place for the people we bring assistance to. Team Rubicon has changed my life, and the future course of it for the better, without a doubt. [2]

In 2010, Clay's marriage ended, and he was unable to continue in college when the VA lost his benefit application papers and payments were delayed for ten months. Frustrated, he lobbied Congress on behalf of veteran's benefits: "You fight for your country, then come home and have to fight against your own country for the benefits you were promised." After he left college, he underwent treatment for depression while staying with his friend Jake, who believes Clay did everything recommended for a successful transition to civilian life. He returned to his hometown of Houston, found a job, and started dating. But this new start failed to save his life.

Those who knew Clay well describe feelings and behaviors that are consistent with moral injury. In January 2007, he deployed to Iraq with the 2nd Battalion, 7th Marine Regiment. Within a month, Clay overheard news that his bunkmate, Blake Howey, had been killed, and afterward, he moved from his upper bed to Blake's lower bunk to be closer to him. But war makes little room for processing such grief. In March 2007, Clay's platoon was ambushed while he was driving a Humvee and unable to shoot his weapon. A sniper killed his close friend, Nathan Windsor, who was walking in front of the vehicle. He questioned why he had not died instead. Three days later, a sniper took out his left wrist, missing his head by a split second when Clay lifted it. "I would've thought you'd feel like the luckiest guy on the earth that you got shot and they missed your head, but that's not how he felt," his father, Stacy Hunt, said. "He felt he didn't deserve it. . . . He could never really leave behind the feeling of, 'Why me? Why did I make it and the other guys didn't?'" Clay was sent back to California for treatment of his wrist and PTSD. There he plunged himself into helping other wounded soldiers recover. Clay felt guilty about leaving his company, and upon recovering, he trained as a sniper and volunteered to go to Afghanistan, where he lost two more friends. His mother, Susan Selke, observed, "When that last one in Afghanistan went down, it just undid him." He kept photos of his four deceased friends near the door of his Houston apartment.

After he left the Marines, he struggled to find a new purpose for his life. Stacy Hunt notes, "I think he was a lot more philosophical about life than a lot of us are . . . trying to search for some inner peace and the meaning of life, what was the most important thing." In Clay's search for meaning, he had difficulty sustaining intimate relationships outside his circle of fellow veterans; his marriage lasted just two years. As a civilian, he volunteered for the frontlines to help veterans re-enter society, working in suicide prevention. He felt betrayed by his government, which sent soldiers to fight and then required them to fight for benefits they were promised.

Clay Hunt was a healthy human being injured by war. He did his best to serve his country with honor and integrity in war, and he learned moral values and service to others from his family, his church, and his community. He played football, read voraciously, and collected turtles, but his mother notes that his high-energy life was the opposite of that of a turtle. When he was filling out an application to transfer colleges, he told his parents he was joining the Marines instead, to become part of something larger than himself. Clay said to his mother, "I want to be given a task and complete and do it well. . . . Give me a mission, put me on the ground, let me go do it." Clay had a tattoo on his arm from J.R.R. Tolkien's *Lord of the Rings*: "Not all those who wander are lost." Somehow, he lost his way on the journey home, and, though he found temporary forms of respite, his way out was death.

Clay's friend Jake was among the many veterans from around the country who attended his funeral. In delivering a eulogy, he said:

> He thought the world was supposed to be a better place than it is, and he lived every day of his life thinking, perhaps naively, that his efforts could make the world be what he thought it should be.... When [Clay] woke up every day and his efforts seemed in vain, that made him more depressed.... Clay, I think that you realize now just how loved you were.... You have a church full of people who are honored to be here, and we love you."[3]

Veterans return from combat to solitary confinement. Some begin their emotional and spiritual isolation in battle as they grieve losses or silently doubt the morality of what they are doing. Others feel it when they come home. Many return locked in a space of inarticulate silence where they cannot find words for the atrocities and terrors they experienced. Haunted by this silent space, they enter a consumption- and entertainment-driven society where people feel purpose and power from self-absorption and bond socially by shopping and not thinking. Veterans not only find themselves bereft of the intense camaraderie and noble meaning that supported them in combat, but they also return to a society full of lonely, purposeless individuals; a declining, desperate middle class; weak communities; and therapy- or healing-driven approaches to moral issues.

Veterans often return to self-imposed and socially imposed pressures to "put the war behind you and move on," or they find their humanity challenged because they served in the military. Perhaps even more alienating is hero worship or the formulaic "thank you for your service" that meets the needs of those unwilling or unable to listen to their complex experiences. We have found in our work with veterans that many do not feel like heroes, but feel, instead, a sense of personal failure or a deep ambivalence about their service in war. After exiting the intense sense of purpose and meaning that war can deliver, veterans may feel duped or disillusioned and reject the meaning systems that made them feel part of something bigger than themselves. In all these ways, combat veterans and the civilians who welcome them home fail to comprehend each other across the deep divides in their separate worlds. Despite the fact that veterans were once and are again part of the civilian world, few lifelines exist to offer them the emotional and spiritual bonds needed to sustain long-term recovery.

Chris Hedges, a graduate of Harvard Divinity School, worked for nearly two decades as a war correspondent, covering a host of conflicts in Central America, the Middle East, Africa, and Eastern Europe that had no clear frontlines or safe areas. He was ambushed on desolate roads, trapped in firefights, taken captive, strafed, shot at, shelled, beaten, and imprisoned. His job was to translate what he saw and experienced into coherent stories so his readers could understand the wars he reported. While unarmed, not trained to kill, and not part of a military company, he experienced the terrors of war firsthand as a keen observer who had to reflect upon what he saw. Rita first met him in the late 1990s after he had left the *New York Times* and was spending a year as a Harvard journalism fellow writing his memoir, *War Is a Force That Gives Us Meaning*. He writes with clarity about a personal sense of failure in combat.

> One of the most difficult realizations of war is how deeply we betray ourselves, how far we are from the image of gallantry and courage we desire, how instinctual and primordial fear is. We do not meditate on action. Our movements are usually motivated by a numbing and overpowering desire for safety.[4]

Because of his searing, honest work on war, we invited Chris to testify at the Truth Commission on Conscience in War. Chris understands the horror and terror that provoke PTSD, but he also probes the dangerous addictions of war. He asserts that war seduces combatants with its powerful elixir of noble purpose and meaning, an elixir that is an antidote to the shallowness of consumer culture and aimless and marginalized lives that matter to few, if anyone. War, he admits, "gives us resolve, a cause. It allows us to be noble."[5]

That belief in a noble cause relies on the cohesion of camaraderie and its shared responsibility and on obedience to the chain of command under the leadership of a superior. Repeated and varied studies of human behavior have shown that the majority of ordinary, good people will override their own moral distress and inflict dangerous levels of electric shocks when someone in authority tells them that they must do so to complete an experiment—this is true without military training. War fuels this human tendency to obey authority with an extraordinary life-or-death urgency, which can shred a person's moral conscience. It usually fails, however, to destroy it completely, though it may lie buried for years before it returns to haunt a veteran of combat.[6]

Moral injury cannot afflict a sociopath. People can carry sociopathic tendencies, but those who carry the disorder in the extreme kill indifferently or for pleasure, and they lack a moral conscience. They ignore laws and social norms, act impulsively and rashly, lack remorse, lie easily, and view others as means to achieve their goals of power. Brain scans of sociopaths indicate they do not register normal emotions, which means they cannot feel joy, love, guilt, or anguish. They can fake such feelings but do not have a capacity to experience them. Their lack of affect can be confused with depression—they are often offered pity and compassion from others unable to detect that their lack of feelings is not the same as being depressed. They do not suffer emotional pain, but inflict it upon others, and some are charismatic enough to entrap people emotionally. They can have a sophisticated intellectual understanding of what others consider right or wrong and be able to manipulate such ideas, but a sociopath chooses actions based on impulse and utility, not moral values. A moral framework of meaning that guides their behavior is irrelevant to them because sociopaths cannot feel the emotional impact of their behavior on others. Their deficiencies also make them less susceptible to PTSD.

Veterans with moral injury have souls in anguish, not a psychological disorder. Feelings of guilt, shame, and contrition were once considered the feelings of a normal ethical person. However, secular approaches tend to view them as psychological neuroses or disorders that inhibit individual self-actualization and interfere with "authentic" feelings and urges. Yet, many veterans do not believe their moral struggles are psychological illnesses needing treatment. Instead, they experience their feelings as a profound spiritual crisis that has changed them, perhaps beyond repair.

The military's masculine culture is often devastating for women. Though they are not officially supposed to serve in combat and did not receive training for it until 1993, wars against insurgencies make women's participation inevitable. The film *Lioness* tells the story of a group of women from various branches of the military who were recruited as "ambassadors" in Iraq to reach out to women and children. They followed a combat unit in order to search captured women. The women soldiers discuss being in combat with men, and one describes being betrayed by a unit leader and having to kill someone.

At its most extreme, military service subjects women to sexual violence at twice the civilian rate. Rape is a far more common source of trauma for women in war than combat and is referred to as military sexual trauma (MST). MST only began to be discussed significantly in public in 2011. According to the 2012 film *The Invisible War*, half a million young women soldiers, 20 percent, have reported being raped. It is estimated that 80 percent of rapes go unreported and only 10 percent of reported rapes are prosecuted, with a 2 percent conviction rate. The punishment for rape is mild to nonexistent. In addition, victims have been denied VA medical benefits for being injured and traumatized during a rape. When a group of victims sued the Department of Defense, their case was dismissed because rape was deemed an "occupational hazard" of military service. Sexual assault can create profound moral dilemmas for women in the military. A woman in combat may find herself taking orders from or needing protection from a sexual predator. If she breaks the camaraderie of her unit by accusing someone of rape, it is not just her life that may be endangered.

Women can also be used in sexist ways for torture. In one case, Alyssa Peterson served with C Company in Military Intelligence in Iraq as an Arabic-speaking interrogator at the prison at Tal Afar airbase. A twenty-seven-year-old devout Mormon, she was put in "the cage," where "enhanced interrogation" techniques included "walling, cigarette burning, punching and being blindfolded naked." The blindfolded captives were humiliated when their blindfolds were removed to show women were present. After two days, Peterson refused to continue with the interrogations. She believed the torture demeaned her to the point that she did not want to live with what she did in the name of serving her country. She shot herself on September 15, 2003. No public media source reported her suicide.[7]

Any person with a conscience feels occasional guilt or shame for something she or he did, but war can require extreme actions that violate the very basis of moral identity. The life or death urgency of war forces untenable actions that can elicit profound guilt or shame. When we feel that what we did was wrong or unforgivable and that our lives and our meaning system no longer make sense, our reason for living is in tatters. This shattering of the soul challenges what holds life together, and the anguish of moral injury begins.

Mac

Mac's eighty-one-year-old grandmother walked barefoot to church through the streets of Brooklyn in every season to ask the Virgin Mary to spare the life of her grandson in Vietnam. Her prayers were answered when Mac came back alive. But he did not feel he could ever go home. The family that loved him deeply and welcomed him back could not fully understand him. "My father was a construction worker, my mother a seamstress in a sweatshop until she died at seventy-five. They loved me, but they really did not know what to do with me," he says. For him, the war never ceased; it was in his head and in his soul.

Shortly after returning from Vietnam, Mac married the young woman to whom he had gotten engaged after deployment. But the man his fiancée married was not the man who left for war. While he was never physically violent, Mac admits he was very hard to live with. One day his mother-in-law took him aside at a family function, looked deeply into his eyes, and asked, "Mac, you are no longer the man you used to be. What happened to you in Vietnam?" He could not give an answer. His marriage lasted barely five years.

Mac felt confused and adrift, like a stranger in his own home. In 1971, he writes in his postwar journals:

> Things were different . . . or maybe I was different. As much as I had come to hate the war, there at least I felt I belonged. I knew what was expected of me, and I had become ruthlessly proficient at fulfilling those expectations. Here I am a misfit, an aberration, isolated and alone.[8]

Since his home was no longer a safe space of belonging, Mac's faith also lost its meaning. He became an atheist.

For the first few years, Mac kept telling himself and his loved ones that he just needed to "chill out" for a while and he would be back to normal, or at least feel better. He would leave New York with his backpack and his dog and hike through the Adirondacks for months. He would often smoke dope and sought to be as solitary as possible. When the first snow arrived, he headed home. Many people tried to help Mac, but they did not really know how. And others made life worse.

> I realized that America had little tolerance, interest, or understanding for its returning warriors. I was called a drug addict and baby killer by many in the general public and ostracized even by fellow veterans from previous wars for being a crybaby and a loser, for lacking dedication and effort, for disgracing the "uniform," ourselves, and the country by contributing to what was widely regarded as America's first lost war. This realization that I was alienated and alone and that no one seemed to understand or care about what I was undergoing made me sad at first. Soon after, that sadness was replaced by anger and resentment.

Because of Mac's training as an educator, one of his friends found him a teaching position in New York. On the day Mac was supposed to start his job, he realized he simply could not bring himself to do it. He just failed to show up. He could not even explain why. It took him a long time to apologize to his friend.

Other well-meaning, concerned people tried to support and challenge Mac. He was told to put the war behind him, set the memories aside, and move on with his life. Still shocked, in pain, guilt-ridden, and horrified by what he had done and experienced, Mac turned inward. Through a process of intense self-reflection, he understood that he could not just put the war out of his mind, and he realized he could not—he must not—put the war aside. It had challenged all that he believed in about the world and about himself. He had to confront the war head on. He could not begin to heal without facing his moral injury and fully acknowledging the moral gravity of his actions in war. And so, he began the long journey to become a philosopher of war.

As a philosopher, Mac challenges modern therapeutic approaches to the suffering of veterans as afflictions of stress and trauma, clustered under the umbrella of PTSD. This view deems moral and spiritual considerations as irrelevant, or even as a hindrance to restoring psychological health. But Mac's own upbringing and personal experience of war led him to believe instead that to deal with the moral anguish generated by war requires taking responsibility for the pain of war. Feelings of guilt, shame, meaninglessness, and alienation come from knowing that one transgressed one's most deeply held beliefs and moral values, and therefore, one's core sense of self. Mac believes these feelings of transgression and remorse must be listened to, acknowledged, and deeply addressed, instead of being dismissed, minimized, and silenced. Veterans who struggle with moral injury are struggling to recover their lost sense of humanity, which they require to reintegrate into the human community. No easy shortcut can bring them home.

Herm

Herm was shipped home and spent six months in Great Lakes Hospital. Unable to use his arms at all, he was wheeled around to meet with other injured soldiers. His own time in combat gave him enormous credibility for counseling and comforting them, but witnessing the war's devastating consequences for men he had come to love only added to his own moral struggles with the war.

Herm's moral struggles took place in a country that had changed considerably during his time in combat. The war had become increasingly unpopular, and negative analyses by politicians, the press, and religious leaders continued to multiply. These analyses influenced the dialogue about the war among young service men and women and had an impact on their behavior:

> The moral anguish of the war in Vietnam presented a new challenge to those who fought. Many found that there was NO EXIT. Even after coming home, the war stayed in our heads, in our hearts, in our horrific dreams, in our loss of sensitivity, and in our difficulties in interpersonal relationships. Untreated post-traumatic shock became an enduring disorder. These hidden wounds still linger in the lives of many veterans.

Herm was especially troubled by the moral failures of those who prosecuted the war. He notes:

> The United States Army emerged from the Vietnam War with battlefield leadership and moral leadership in a body bag. Senior non-commissioned officers remained on firebases or in base camps while sergeants first class led squads and platoons into battle. Their own troops used fragmentation grenades against incompetent officers, and the bonds of loyalty and obedience between a leader and those he was supposed to lead were cut by soldiers who murdered him.

The conscientious objector laws and directives of the military protected only those who belonged to pacifist religious traditions. Whether draftees or volunteers, soldiers who judged this war unjust and immoral had no legal way to resist. Watching them go to jail rather than fight was heart rending.

So was watching those who fought.

I am tormented to this day remembering the soldiers who tried hard not to kill, even while they were conscious of their obligation to protect their fellow soldiers. I watched their moral sensitivity erode. I was haunted by something one of my seminary professors told me, "to violate your conscience is to commit moral suicide."

When Herm was released from the hospital and returned to his family, not only had he never seen his new son but he could not even hold him. The first time he had his nine-month-old son in his lap, his arms were in huge white casts, and the child was terrified. His wife, Ardis, a professional nurse, bore the exhausting work of taking care of both an infant and a traumatized and helpless husband. A husband who had once provided for his wife returned unprepared to cope with being totally dependent on her, while also being emotionally isolated from her.

I could not feed myself, bathe myself, or even use the toilet myself, nothing. Instead of returning to my role as her husband, I became my wife's other baby. In addition to having a hard time being so helpless, I also had survivor guilt and nightmares. I could not relate to what my family was doing at home; I was disinterested in their conversations and daily activities. I felt a misfit with my family and, though I was in our house, I did not feel at home.

For all the pain and time of dealing with my injuries, I benefited from having to go back to the hospital for regular treatment sessions. Unlike many veterans who returned to small towns or communities with few or no combat veterans, I had the recurring company of others like myself. I felt truly at home only with other wounded soldiers—they alone understood my struggle to return to stateside life. The VA lacked information on PTSD, so no one really knew what to do for those of us who came home from Vietnam. Also, for soldiers, it was a sign of weakness to admit to being depressed and traumatized. So, we told our stories to each other and tried to come to terms with our hidden wounds that way.

Veterans of war are a close-knit community because we know there are things others cannot understand that we don't have to explain to each other. But that closeness of vets is hard on families. You have so many responsibilities to your family to fulfill that you don't want to burden them with things that you feel are shameful or that might unleash too much pain. It's easy to shut your wife out and to disclose nothing because it feels overwhelming to make yourself so vulnerable to someone you are supposed to be strong for.

Because of the damage to his arms, the military considered releasing Herm from the service. But Herm wanted to stay, and he worked extra hard at his first assignment as a hospital chaplain in order to prove he was fit to remain in the military. This work took him away from home a great deal, and though he was able to spend more time with Ardis and his son later, the first year was especially difficult.

Pamela

When Dweylon came home, he spent eighteen months on a base in New York and was transferred to Georgia before he left the Army. First, he lived with his girlfriend for six months and then moved in with his father near Atlanta while he started college. He struggled with anger at the authorities that launched an illegal, unjust war and forced him to fight it, and he lived on edge, thinking about what he had done:

I remember coming back to the states and having faceless and nameless civilians cheering and clapping at us. I thought, "What the hell are you clapping about?" I know people were trying to show appreciation, but when you are coming home from where nothing good happened to you or anyone over there, there is nothing to clap about or smile about or celebrate. Nothing at all. This is war. Everybody thinks they are right in a war, but everyone still dies in the end. There's nothing good about it.

Though he never had to fire a weapon and kill someone, Dweylon believes that he is as morally culpable of killing innocent people as those who did:

I don't want to equate what I did to those who had to kill people. I know I cannot imagine having to do that, to stare down your gun at someone, squeeze the trigger, and see them dead—to have the courage to do that and then to adjust to this when you come home. When I think about my own role, it messes with me, because I didn't squeeze a trigger but I did the same thing.

Dweylon accepts that his role in an immoral war was the same as those who did the killing. He thinks about it a lot, but he finds it hard to talk about.

Pamela understands the very real threats her son faced every day. She continues to worry about him and the lack of help he is getting from the VA.

What he has achieved at home is especially miraculous in the face of VA services that are not only just awful but also require veterans to have to fight their own government for the disability support or financial compensation owed them from serving in war. It can take many years going back and forth filing and responding to documents for disability pay. Some even have to hire an attorney to help them make their way through all the red tape. And if you can get an appointment to see a specialist to discuss options for psychological treatment, you might have to wait many hours, which means, if you work, you have to take a whole day off. In this job market, that can mean having to choose between a job and treatment. Dweylon came back from war eight years ago, and he has still not received help for his PTSD. A general physician gave him drugs, but he didn't like them, and I know the major drugs of choice for veterans who can't get care are weed or alcohol. I am not convinced that Dweylon has not used weed and I do know that he has had some run-ins with the police since his return. But despite all this, I want to help Dweylon avoid those addictions, which are so devastating to people's lives. That is another reason I look after him. I owe him that as his mother and out of respect for his military service.

When Dweylon reflects on how war changed him, he knows he still feels angry about how people view those in military service who are responsible for protecting their freedom. While Iraq was immoral in his view, not all wars are, and as long as someone has to fight to protect people, they should not say awful things about soldiers. They should understand what war did, not just to the Iraqi people but also to the United States in being part of something that was wrong from the beginning, but which most people just ignored as they went on with their lives for so many years.

Other things sit deep in his soul and haunt him.

I am unresolved about death. The military encouraged us to feel glory, to shoot to kill, and to love it, but I wasn't feeling any of that too much. I think of the countless bodies of innocent people who didn't want to be involved in a war—babies, children, people who were just in the wrong place at the wrong time. Wearing that uniform, carrying my rifle, and doing what we did is not something I am proud of. I was representing one of the biggest purveyors of violence in the world, the U.S., a country that was founded on violence. I love my country, but no one should be proud of an unnecessary war. There were so many people who got killed and didn't need to get killed, a child and his mother who got up one morning, went out to get some water, and were shot or blown up—so many dead innocent people like that. They stay with you; you can't shake them off or ignore them.

Camilo

Camilo's travel from Iraq lasted four days. His commercial flight home was a strange experience. For the first time in a long while, he did not have to dodge bullets or worry about grenades. At the first stop, Al Asad Air Base in Iraq, departing soldiers received two briefings from a chaplain on readjusting to home and on suicide prevention. Rather than really helping, Camilo thought the briefings were designed to protect the Army's image.

> A twenty-minute session centering on the admonition *Don't commit suicide* doesn't do much to ease the anguish of a soldier dealing with the horror, for instance, of having killed a child, just as a group session with a combat stress team isn't much help if your life is at risk twenty-four hours a day.[9]

During a two-hour stay in Germany, he was advised not to wear his uniform at home because he and his family could be targeted by terrorists and not to drink and drive. Arriving in Baltimore brought him relief and happiness, but to get home to Florida, he had to pay the fare himself, a military policy. On the final, self-funded leg of his flight, Camilo's feelings shifted and became more complex:

> As I transferred to a plane that would take me to Florida, I found my mood alternating between joy and melancholy. I knew I was happy because I was going to see my daughter and my family again, but it was less clear why I was also sad. Perhaps it was because I had to return to a war and an occupation I hated. Or it might have been the secret certainty that I would not return, and that I

was leaving the men of my unit behind in a war where we did not belong but also in a land where we had created a brotherhood that can only flourish amid the horror of war.[10]

Camilo was also apprehensive about seeing his mother. Communications between them had been hard. As he remarks, "trying to keep my cool during combat missions was not easy, but it was nothing compared to the self-control required to keep calm while talking to my mother on the phone." Camilo's mother was distraught by his involvement in a war that she considered illegal and immoral. She believed the Iraqi insurgents had the right to fight the U.S. occupation, and she was terrified for her son's life. Camilo felt guilty and ashamed for having put his mother in that heart-wrenching situation. He did not know what to expect from their first reunion and was very anxious about her reactions. But when he arrived at her apartment, she just ran to him, hugged him tightly, sobbed uncontrollably, and kissed his hair. They stood like that for a long time, in silence, their eyes filled with tears.

The following morning, Camilo was to see his daughter Samantha. Hoping she would still remember him, he started questioning his ability to be a good father after what he had done in war. He had abused prisoners, knowing it was wrong, but he lacked the courage to speak out:

> How could I ever teach my daughter right from wrong when I had done so wrong myself? What moral authority did I have left to be a good father? As our time in Iraq continued and I become more and more preoccupied with the single task of surviving, these issues concerned me less and less. But now, at the door of Samantha's home, they all came flooding back to me.[11]

Samantha, barely four, did recognize him. It was not too late to be a good father. Reconnecting deeply with his daughter strengthened Camilo's resolve to do everything in his power to fight the military red tape that had kept him unfairly in Iraq. The hours of his two-week leave sped by too fast, as Camilo made phone calls and tacked back and forth between different offices. Master Sergeant Wingard from the Florida National Guard confirmed that, as a non-citizen, Camilo's contract had been mistakenly extended after its eight years and he was supposed to be discharged. In a terrible catch-22, Camilo had to be back in Iraq in order to be discharged. If he did not follow this procedure at the end of his leave, Sergeant Wingard said he would be considered AWOL, "absent without leave."

When Camilo challenged this conundrum, Sergeant Wingard finally admitted that there was no such rule. Camilo's commander could sign the papers from Iraq, so Camilo wrote to Captain Werfel immediately explaining his request. His captain issued an angry refusal and charged Camilo with being disrespectful and a coward. Having already lost a week trying to be discharged, he contacted the next officer in the line of command, restating his whole case in greater detail and quoting the appropriate regulation. Lieutenant Colonel Mirable was more courteous, but after a three-day wait, he ordered Camilo to return to his unit until the end of its mission.

Camilo felt deflated. He had still naively believed that by following regulations and procedure, his case would be treated fairly. What was he supposed to do now? "I had to go back to Iraq, brutalize the people, rape the land, and possibly die there, all against my conscience."[12] He was afraid that if he went back, he would lose his soul and never be human again. He could no longer be a father to Samantha. Camilo's mother insisted that he should not go back and that many people would support his stance, and she gave him the names of organizations that would help him. Yet the decision was agonizing. If Camilo went AWOL, he would have to face court martial and go to jail. A harsh sentence would mean that Samantha would lose her father anyway. If he played it safe, Camilo could hope to come back alive from war, keep his career intact, and go on with his life. But, he thought, what about the Iraqis?

Memories of his Iraq days came flooding back: the man Camilo killed reflexively, even though he was too far away to pose a real danger; the child near the headless corpse of his father; the civilians killed near a beautiful mosque; the man he shot in the car. Were these memories and images real? Camilo knew they were, but he could not remember clearly. The night before his departure for Iraq, Camilo went to bed but did not sleep at all. When the time came to arise, he could not move. Hours passed. He missed his plane and fell asleep. When he woke up, he thought he should catch the next plane, but fell asleep again. Finally he woke up and knew he could not go back to Iraq.

Going AWOL meant that Camilo had to leave and go into hiding. He left for the Northeast, spoke to the press about what he had experienced in Iraq, and connected with several organizations that wanted to support him. He applied for CO status. At the same time, even though he was far from Iraq and had renounced the use of violence, Camilo knew the war was not really over for him.

> This would be, first and foremost, a war waged within myself, one where my fears and doubts would come face to face with my conscience, a war to reclaim my humanity and my spiritual freedom.[13]

Memories of combat, previously repressed, flooded to the surface.

After months hiding while he went through a difficult process of trying to sort out what he should do, Camilo went public with his opposition to the war and turned himself in to the authorities. His mother and his family supported him. In his interview on 60 Minutes, included in Soldiers of Conscience, Camilo claimed:

> This is not a good war, the reasons that took us to war were not true, there were no weapons of mass destruction, no link between Saddam and Al Qaeda. The Iraqis don't like you and people don't want you in Iraq: no military contact and no military duty is going to justify being part of that war.[14]

Camilo was the first enlisted soldier from Iraq to go public with his condemnation of the war and to refuse to redeploy. His application for conscientious objector status has never been denied or granted. Arrested at his reappearance press conference, he was court-martialed and sentenced to a year in prison. Yet he claimed he never felt freer, as "there is no higher exertion of your freedom than to follow your conscience."[15] Amnesty International declared him a prisoner of conscience. He served nine months in prison and was given a bad conduct discharge.

WHEN KEVIN BENDERMAN was ordered to redeploy to Iraq, he realized, like Camilo, that he could not go back. After a decade in military service in a family that honored such service, and despite earning multiple medals for his six-month tour in Iraq, he had reached a line he could not cross. He applied for conscientious objector status. In the application, he had to include an interview with a chaplain who could verify that his opposition to war in any form was sincere, not an attempt to escape war duty, and that he had clearly had a crystallization of conscience against war. The first chaplain he asked refused, and then, after the chaplain deployed to Kuwait, he e-mailed Kevin to tell him he was ashamed of him. The second chaplain, who understood the CO process and did the interview, concluded that Kevin was sincere and that "his lifestyle is congruent with his claim of conscientious objection." In his seven-page application, Kevin wrote, "War is the greatest form of wrong. . . . I believe that my moral obligation to humanity is to not allow myself to be a part of this destruction." He submitted the application in December 2004, but it was eventually denied. When his unit was deployed in February 2005, he chose not to go with them. Kevin was arrested and tried for desertion and failure to report for deployment. He was court-martialed on July 5, demoted from sergeant to private, given a dishonorable discharge, and sentenced to fifteen months in military prison for not deploying with his company.

The United States Army decided to imprison me as a result of my recognizing the Truth and speaking out about it. I want the people responsible for that to know that I consider it an honor to be jailed for telling the Truth—far better than to be condemned to Hell for following a blatant lie that would result in my being an accomplice to such an atrocity.[16]

In his Truth Commission testimony, Tyler Boudreau described his return in terms of dislocation, with his body at home and his head in Iraq. Addicted to war, he spent many predawn hours online seeking bad news about the war and especially wanting to feel back in battle and to feel the pain of it. Of his private torment, he asserts,

They say war is hell, but I say it's the foyer to hell. I say coming home is hell, and hell ain't got no coordinates. You can't find it on the charts, because there are no charts. Hell is no place at all, so when you're there, you're nowhere—you're lost. The narrative, that's your chart, your own story. There are guys who come home from war and live fifty years without a narrative, fifty years lost. They don't know their own story, never have, and never will. But they're moving amidst the text every day and every long night without even realizing it. . . . They live inside the narrative like a cell, and their only escape is to understand its dimensions.[17]

Tyler wanted to be two different men. One would be the glorious, successful commander, the other needed to scream, "This shit ain't right!" and start a new life. Tyler's internal struggle was so intense that it was physically painful. He wondered how much he had forfeited his own judgment to pursue his teenage dreams of glory, his idealistic views of war, and the prize of being a Marine and a commander. After serving his entire adult life as a Marine, he realized he could not return to Iraq. He resigned his commission and left the Corps, which required him to change everything about his life, from his friends to his daily activities. In his memoir, Tyler notes that if a war seems just, the individual moral burden is shared with all who fight it and the leaders who declare it. However, if a veteran decides a war is unjust and immoral and rejects the government or cause used to justify it, he faces his moral burden, his every act of war, in full and alone, without excuses: "To cite the lies and the deceptions and the propaganda and the manipulation—true as it all might be—only makes the pack more ponderous."[18]

In accepting that burden, Tyler had a painful revelation: he had always had the information and the rational ability to be critical of the war in Iraq and his role in the Marines. He simply decided to ignore the facts and reject his critical judgment: "I should have known better. Instead, I chose to ignore the facts and to ride blithely through the fantasy without critique. Now, I must pack the load alone."[19] Tyler realized that if he tried to justify his part in the war or gloss over the gravity of what he did, he would only be in another form of denial. Instead, he chose to carry this burden.

> Many veterans . . . let their conscience and their guilt do quiet battle for years, and while they may not hear the shouting, they can feel the turmoil in their guts. The only way, so far as I can tell, to stop the incessant quarrel is to own the responsibility. If I own it, I can disown it. That is the only way to truly unload my pack.[20]

Tyler moved from this moment of self-revelation to a process of rigorous introspection and disclosure. But he also realized that introspection is not enough; withdrawal can become denial. Disclosing thoughts to family, to friends, to a community, or to a wider public is essential to shedding greater light on the depths of hell and to unpacking, slowly, his load.

IN THE STRUGGLE FOR truth and meaning after war, the surest testimonies to the intractable presence of soul, of moral conscience, are those who rediscover it and struggle to repair it after the worst thing ever devised by human beings to destroy it. The hard-won victories of self-possession—such as the decision to go to prison rather than return to war, the fleeting moments of self-disclosure to friends, the reawakening of a sense of purpose—these gradual signs of recovery, born of honesty, patient listening, and personal courage, are not achieved by "putting the war behind you and moving on." Easy to discourage, difficult to hold, these precious life-sustaining insights and inclinations become, eventually, the small gifts of spirit that begin to breathe life back into a soul shattered by war. And, thus, the long journey begins.

4

I Will Live with Moral Injury
the Rest of My Life

> Prepare, my friends, the knight's return,
> And pray we are not too blind to learn.
>
> CAMILLO C. "MAC" BICA, philosopher
> of war, former U.S. Marine Captain, and
> Vietnam veteran

Veterans often yearn for the pure and selfless love they shared in battle. Returning to the civilian world is an emotionally wrenching struggle that is akin to ending an all-consuming romantic love. Ancient mythologies understand the fusion of love and war and its dangers. In Homer's *Odyssey*, Aphrodite, the goddess of love, and Ares, the god of war, had a long, illicit affair. Ares had failed to win the contest to marry Aphrodite because he relied on his warrior strength. Instead, the lame metalsmith Hephaestus won her through his wits and then exacted his revenge for her adulterous affair by trapping the lovers together.

> You will see the pair of lovers now as they lie embracing in my bed; the sight of them makes me sick at heart. Yet I doubt their desire

to rest there longer, fond as they are. They will soon unwish their posture there; but my cunning chains shall hold them both fast.

The pressure-cooker of battle compresses the arguments and idiosyncrasies of individuals into a single fighting unit, committed to one purpose and to each other. Personal survival is intertwined with the survival of the unit. If a soldier fails his duty, he will be responsible for the deaths of his friends and live with the shame of his failure to save them for the rest of his life. As journalist Sebastian Junger notes:

> The classic story of a man throwing himself on a hand grenade— certain death, but an action that will almost certainly save everyone else—is neither a Hollywood cliché nor something that only happened in wars gone by. It is something that happens with regularity, and I don't think it can be explained by "army training" or any kind of suicidal impulse. I think that kind of courage goes to the heart of what it means to be human and to affiliate with others in a kind of transcendent way. Of course, once you have experienced a bond like that, everything else looks pathetic and uninteresting. That may be one reason combat vets have such a hard time returning to society.[1]

Rarely, if ever in ordinary life are people required to focus, with such purity, everything in them—mind, emotions, physical strength, perception, and skill—on the present moment with so many others. In ordinary life, standards of masculinity tend to prevent such intense self-transcending, absorbing bonding among men or between men and women, except in the consuming throes of early romance.

Euphoria is addicting and self-sacrifice is transcending; but equilibrium is life-sustaining and reciprocity is the heart of love. Veterans who seek friendships with former comrades can be disappointed in the long run because battlefield relationships are built on intense danger; on a rapidly induced, temporary construction of unity; and on constraints on emotional vulnerability. Combat forms a tightly closed circle of insiders and outsiders, insiders for whom one is willing to die and outsiders who will never understand the horrific conditions under which that willingness was tested. Once the pressures of combat and a shared purpose disappear, the thinness of camaraderie can disappoint, and moral qualms can corrode unquestioned solidarity. Eventually, cultural, ethical, and political differences can fray the nostalgia of war memories, even when emotional chains make turning to other relationships nigh impossible.

In war, the intrusion of civilian life can make fighting more difficult. Soldiers must sharply divide their souls between those they love and those they are supposed to kill. In the days before cell phones and the Internet, the battlefield was a sealed world, invaded only briefly and infrequently by letters from home. Now, family and friends at home can speak directly from a screen or a phone to anywhere in the world. Despite this increase in access, contact is still controlled and limited. Loved ones can wait months for news from their soldiers. Even when the news is good, constant reminders of home can split a soldier's soul in a war against an insurgency that involves mothers and children. Empathy makes moral conscience possible, and it can undermine the will to kill. Camilo describes in chapter 3 how thinking of his daughter Samantha disrupted his willingness to fight and led him to experience the humanity of the Iraqi people. Dweylon struggled with the plight of ordinary people in Iraq, certain that most of the people killed were innocent civilians. Kevin saw the suffering of the Iraqi people, came to understand their religious commitments, and witnessed the dehumanization of soldiers, which turned him against war altogether. When Joshua saw in a Saudi jihadist a man like himself and wanted to imagine a different world in which they could talk to each other, he could no longer do his job.

Battle camaraderie cannot hold the complexities of whole persons. The transition from war camaraderie to life-sustaining, intimate relationships requires withdrawal from an addiction to the drama of combat and a transition to ordinary life: doing daily chores, going to work every day, and forming emotionally open, complicated relationships with family and friends. The journey back is a jagged, arduous route on treacherous trails, marked by switchbacks and occasional dead ends. It proceeds by small stubborn steps forward that replace the battle camaraderie of soldiers with life-sustaining love.

Mac

Five years after coming home to New York in 1970, Mac had to admit to himself that the strategy of just "chilling out" was not enough to help him to go back, if not to his old life, at least to a meaningful life. Mac started attending meetings at a VA hospital, and he quickly began volunteering for a number of projects and groups. The situation was desperate. The VA was not prepared to help all the veterans in emotional pain and deep anguish. In the early days, about all the help the VA offered was some group therapy and heavy medication like Thorazine to ease depression and anxiety. After seeing the effects of drug therapy on many young men, Mac promised himself he would never accept "zombie-fication." He still shivers in horror at the memory of the veterans walking the hallways of the VA hospitals with empty gazes, dragging their feet:

> After several years of isolation and denial, trying to avoid "contaminating" friends and family, and the stigma of being a Vietnam veteran, I was convinced by another vet to seek help at the Veterans Administration (VA). Almost immediately, I was assailed by VA clinicians who "diagnosed" my inability to cope, alienation, nightmares, etcetera as personal inadequacy and weakness, probably due to some preexisting condition, perhaps a personality disorder, maybe even schizophrenia. Most likely, they hypothesized, my difficulties had something to do with my mother being overweight or my being toilet-trained too early. What was peculiarly absent from all this analysis and testing and the ad hominem attacks, however, was any reference to the war. So, I blamed myself for my weakness and my mother for her eating habits and for how

she raised me, and resigned myself to the fact that, for all intents and purposes, at twenty-five, my life was over. Was I crazy, a baby killer, a crybaby, a coward? Perhaps I was all of these. Needless to say, I wasn't very pleased with myself, with those around me, or with the fact that, other than a heavy regimen of Thorazine, what some refer to as a "chemical lobotomy," VA doctors and clinicians weren't offering much help and guidance. So, it became apparent to me that if I was going to salvage what remained of my life—and I was not at all sure healing was possible—I needed to do it myself, to come to an understanding, perhaps even an acceptance, of what I had done and what I'd become.

Mac tried group therapy where, angry and in emotional pain, he unleashed his feelings on the therapists. He remembers his outbursts made a young intern, Kristen, cry a few times. But she always returned to lead the group. Once the therapy sessions ended, Kristen asked Mac if they could stay in touch. Mac was very surprised: "Why, after I treated you so badly and I made your life miserable for months?" Kristen told him that she had learned to really care for him and was hoping they could become friends. They did indeed build an important friendship and remain close friends today.

In reflecting on those days at the VA, Mac thinks that Kristen saved his life, not as a therapist, but as his friend. Kristen helped Mac to get a position teaching philosophy at New York's School of Visual Arts and introduced him to her friends who taught there. She brought him into an intellectual community where he could use his gifts, thrive, and continue to confront the demons of war within him. His supervisors understood that, as Mac puts it, he "needed his space."

During his time recovering at the VA, Mac often felt veterans were at war with the institution. They had to fight to feel visible, to get an answer to even the smallest requests. In order to talk with each other without "supervision," veterans had to organize secret meetings in the cafeteria or in the offices after they closed at night. They made slow progress. Eventually, many self-organized groups obtained meeting space:

> As a result, together with a number of other veterans at the VA in Brooklyn, we began what we called the "Hootch Program," a place of safety—a room in the VA—where vets could sit, drink coffee, and *safely* discuss with each other what was on our minds, mostly how the VA could care less about treating us and how the war had fucked us up. As we became more organized, I became the coordinator of the program, assuming responsibility again, something I vowed never again to do. We began self-help rap groups, AA and NA groups, a Big Brother Program, a vet literacy program, a child-safety fingerprint program, therapeutic trips to the Vietnam Veteran Memorial in D.C., vet art shows and poetry writing and reading workshops, and many other activities, groups, and programs intended to provide the vets with a means of restoring their sense of self-esteem and respect. It proved a very beneficial endeavor for all involved and a model for many similar programs that sprung up at other VAs over the country.

Mac spent so many hours at the VA hospital counseling other vets that it became his home. In the middle of the night, he often received calls to offer peer support in emergencies. Usually, a veteran was about to commit suicide. He ran across the city many nights to stop a hand with a weapon, to soothe a broken spirit, to grasp someone before they leaped from a bridge. Once he was too late. As he extended his hand, the man jumped. Another time he was called to mediate a hostage situation. A desperate, angry, suicidal veteran had sequestered several people. Mac asked the police to let him enter the building unarmed. He asked the veteran if he could talk to him wearing only a small pin that identified him as a Vietnam vet. The two of them paced the hallway, going in circles, until Mac finally convinced the man to release the hostages and to follow him to the VA hospital. The incensed police insisted Mac was not following proper procedure, but reluctantly let the plan proceed. This veteran started therapy and joined several support groups, which eventually enabled him to rebuild a life for himself.

Because of Mac's incredible commitment and gifts, the VA administration offered him a permanent position. While Mac needed the income, he didn't want to lose his independence or his ability to criticize and fight the system, and so he refused. Still, the VA hospital remained Mac's home. He spent most of his days there. And while the doctors and psychologists who worked long hours could leave and go home, Mac knew that he could never go "home," even when he left. War and its aftermath remained within him.

Mac is torn about what to tell young veterans. He feels he will never fully recover from war:

> Vietnam was the defining experience of my life. Though physical wounds may heal, the psychological, emotional, and moral injuries of war linger and fester. Vietnam forever pervades my existence, condemning me to continually relive and question the past. "Did I do enough?" "Could I have done better?" "Did I make the correct decisions?" Inevitable concerns of those who must take life and whose decisions cause others to die. Despite the urging of well-meaning friends and loved ones, I can never forget Vietnam nor put it behind me. No one truly "recovers" from war. No one is ever made whole again. The best that can be hoped, I think, is to achieve a degree of benign acceptance. To that end, I strive each day to forgive and absolve myself of guilt, and to live with the wounds of war that will never heal.

LIKE MAC, TYLER BOUDREAU stewed in the hell of return for a long time. At times, he feels sad about all the time he spent in the military, focused on killing, which is "mentioned so frequently, and with such nonchalance or even zeal, that it becomes a completely acceptable element of every soldier's consciousness." In the struggle to survive war, he knows:

Soldiers . . . push the humanity out of the enemy and out of themselves and soon become mere bodies of instinct and survival. What
is often discovered only later, sometimes too late, is that one's humanity can be quite difficult to recover once it's been evicted. . . .

Coming home has been more than just adapting to life in
the aftermath of war; it has been very much about remaking myself. . . . All of my life's experiences have shaped my identity and
perspectives but war, I think, has made a disproportionate claim
on me.[2]

When Tyler began to recover, he got busy. In 2008, he traveled
to Amman, Jordan, to work on the Iraqi refugee crisis. In 2009, he
cycled across the United States, dropping in on discussions about the
war along the way. He found a deep sense of community and mutual
support in communities of veterans. At home, he became intensely involved in peace activism. He spoke at community events and schools;
he helped organize a collaborative art project with Iraqi immigrants
in New York; he went back to graduate school; and he reengaged as
a father, reconnecting with his two young sons. He even took up
gardening:

Digging in has always been, for me, about killing or keeping myself from being killed. In war, soldiers score the earth with their
shovels, some of them essentially digging their own graves. The
first time I pressed the heel of my boot at home on a garden spade
I felt the shift inside me like tectonic plates beneath the surface.
As I dug into the soil with my fingers, pulling out the rocks and the
roots and preparing it for sowing, I felt the ground in an entirely
different way. The act of digging as creation rather than destruction has been deeply stirring to me. And I don't believe it is simply
that gardening work is engrossing or even that it is rewarding. It
is both, certainly, but there's something more. The entire process
of growing from digging in to harvest is perfectly representative of
the life cycle. All species struggle, in their own manner, to sustain

themselves. It is the natural and logical pattern of existence. Only the human race works so hard to destroy itself.[3]

For so many, the company of other veterans remains a lifelong support system. They offer each other spaces to share what they cannot say to their families or friends, and they find people who understand how to support each other when no one else knows what to do. The challenge for civilians is to respect such friendships, while, at the same time, to offer ties to life beyond those circles and different relationships for the world in which veterans now need to survive. Often, a job and family are not enough. A sense of life purpose and a need to be of service to others are also important. After seeing and inflicting so much suffering on other human beings, being able to make a positive difference in the world, not just with other veterans but also with the civilian world closes a circle of meaning shattered by war.

Herm

On Herm's return from Vietnam, he repaired family relationships that were ruptured by his difficulties adjusting to life at home. He came to understand what his wife, Ardis, went through in his absence, the ways she learned to cope with worry and take care of things he had done before. He also eventually saw the weight of work she faced after he came home feeling dislocated, helpless, and alien. He sought to be more attentive to her needs and feelings, to apologize for outbursts of anger and frustration, and to spend time with his son. He has been able to use what he learned in counseling soldiers returning from war who struggle with family life.

Herm eventually told Ardis about some of his difficult experiences in Vietnam. He told her about the medical procedures he had to do and the kind of injuries he treated during the long night when he was shocked awake by an attack that gave him a concussion. He described how the grenade attack had punctured his sleeping mattress and injured him. His buddy who shared the foxhole and was too injured to get up offered Herm his flak jacket for protection. One of Herm's gifts is a sense of humor, and in telling Ardis about this harrowing experience of war, he ended the story with the reaction of the officers who met in the morning to debrief. Exhausted, he entered the room still wearing the flak jacket. Everyone immediately roared with laughter. It was not until someone pointed to the area under the jacket that Herm understood. He was naked below the jacket. Ardis also recounts with affection a moment when a woman from church asked Herm what he was thinking as he plummeted out of the helicopter. She expected something like a prayer or other religious thoughts. Herm replied, "I thought: Oh, shit!"

Herm has done his best to become the husband and father he wants his family to have, and he has also accepted that his family will never really understand what he went through:

> The physical pains from my wounds continue to remind me of the cost of war. I am never pain free. When those pains seep into my sleep, I have some terrible dreams. Many dreams remind me of the complete loss of independence I had after the fall from the helicopter. And though I have done my best to repair harm to my marriage, I know that war is never something that is left on the battlefield; it always comes home to haunt the families of those who fight.

Because of what he witnessed on the battlefield, his own struggle to serve in a war he believed was unjust, and his disgust at the behavior of so many senior officers, Herm has committed his entire career since Vietnam to creating better protections for the moral consciences of soldiers. As one dimension of that work, he has doggedly pursued the right of selective conscientious objection for those in the armed forces, which would allow proponents of principles of just war to object to a particular war:

> Vietnam left me with both visible and hidden wounds of war; I felt betrayed by the government, the military leadership, the

"military-industrial public press" and my faith community. I continue to feel the pain of returning to a hostile public that did not honor my service to my country and to an indifferent religious community. The Vietnam War remains an example to me of poor moral leadership in both civilian and military leaders. But I made a pledge to stay in military service to help heal the internal problems from inside the institution's walls.

My war experience emboldened me to speak about moral issues to my superiors throughout the rest of my military career. I tried a number of times to push the Department of Defense to allow for selective conscientious objection, which would honor the moral consciences of those who volunteer for military service, who represent the vast majority of religious people. It would allow them to apply the moral principles that the military itself teaches and that are part of the international codes of conduct in war that protect our own soldiers and that govern the U.S. as a member of the United Nations. I felt that by the time I retired, I had done the best that I could do as a moral agent in the system.

As a chaplain endorser for his denomination for eight years after he retired, Herm approved those ordained for military service and oversaw their conduct. His fellow chaplains nominated him to receive the Association of Professional Chaplains 2010 Distinguished Service Award for promoting and exemplifying the standards of professional chaplaincy. He was the first chaplain endorser ever to receive this award:

I am constantly amazed that the people to whom chaplains minister continue to trust us with their stories, opening themselves in conversations both painful and prideful; complex in their simplicity and simple in their complexity; wonderful and terrible stories that reveal the vulnerability and resiliency of the human spirit. They share their life stories with us and welcome us into their narrative, allowing us to interpret their stories with them. I hope and pray that people will feel as awed by being invited into such conversations as I do.

At his alma mater, Calvin College, Herm meets weekly with a group of a dozen men, retired professors from a number of departments. Some are veterans. They sit in a tight circle in the small break lounge, sip coffee, share updates, and check in with each other about what they are working on, what has happened since they were last together, and how they are doing. Herm's fondness for this group lights up his face when he talks about them. When Rita visited him in July 2011 in Grand Rapids, Herm invited her to visit the group, and she found them warm and welcoming. The group's interactions were lightly peppered with good-humored teasing. The conversation that day about the American myth of regeneration through violence proposed by historian Richard Slotkin was intellectually acute and lively.

Two years ago, at one of their sessions, Herm brought up the term *moral injury* and his determination to educate the public about how it may be a factor in veteran suicides. The entire group's general response was, "Why haven't we known about this, and why aren't we doing something about it?" It comes up in the group often now as a topic of conversation. The idea made so much sense to them that they supported Herm when he decided to start an initiative at the Calvin Institute of Christian Worship, which has begun work on moral injury. He also spends some of his time as codirector of the new Soul Repair Center at Brite Divinity School.

Though Herm began his military service as a regular soldier trained to kill, he chose to return to military service to protect moral conscience and minister to soldiers forced to fight a war they believed was immoral and unjust. He received encouragement and support for this work from his professors and his religious community, a circle of friendships he maintains to this day. One of the most dangerous aspects of moral injury is the collapse of meaning and the loss of a will to live. What Herm learned early on was that his faith could offer moral meaning to soldiers in war through a simple Eucharist and the reading of a Psalm, which offer formal and collective recognition of shame, contrition, and grief. In the middle of the most desecrating, dehumanizing situations human beings have ever devised, Herm offered a sacred space and time that held the soul of soldiers in a moment outside of secular history and reminded them of a humanity they shared across the ages. Through the liturgical practices of his ministry, he was able to offer prayers for deliverance, understanding, forgiveness, and moral guidance.

JOSHUA CASTEEL ALSO discovered the capacity of a long moral and religious tradition to touch his soul and lift him out of his private isolation and despair. He and Rita first met when he spoke at Starr King School in Berkeley, California, right after he left the military. At that lecture, Joshua spoke of his moral struggle to reconcile his evangelical faith in Jesus Christ with the patriotic fervor of his Republican convictions. The conflict tore at his soul while he was forced in Iraq to interrogate, repeatedly, prisoners that he knew were innocent. His evangelical faith required him to pray using his own sincere, heartfelt words. He found, in his anguish, he had no words for what he was experiencing. He could not pray. He spoke with a chaplain who gave him a Catholic book of prayer. Joshua was stunned to find prayers written centuries before by strangers who spoke movingly of his dilemma and asked God for mercy and guidance. When he could not speak his own prayers, he found comfort in those of others who suffered as he did. He began to attend Mass every day, and, after his failed interrogation of a jihadist, he made his decision to begin the agonizing return home to a society oblivious to the cost of war. Like Herm, Joshua has continued to find meaning in his faith and in the support of his family and community.

Pamela

Pamela's son Dweylon believes that the bonds he formed with men in his unit remain special. The good soldiers he knew were amazing men and women, willing to do their jobs well and still help out others. They worked very hard as a team. He describes their love as like that in a very close, tight family. He still misses the irreplaceable camaraderie and the intense, incredible feelings he had for other soldiers. Some of the relationships have deepened since they came home. One of his old squad members lives nearby, and Dweylon often visits. When he had a daughter, he made Dweylon the girl's godfather. Dweylon loves the bonds he formed and believes they are unmatched in civilian life. Still, he has needed the help and support of his family and friends to make the slow transition back to civilian life:

> If it had not been the prayers and support of my family and friends, I would have not been able to cope. I knew I took part in something I didn't believe in that was a run for the money. I felt something was wrong from the beginning, but only after I got home and started researching the war, did I realize more and more how it was supported by lies like weapons of mass destruction. If I didn't have people in my family who knew military life, I would never have been able to talk about what I went through over there. I would never have made it alone. I'd have been on the street or dead. I still can't measure the difference they made because it's not over for me. They still have to call and check in with me. I'm really grateful for their persistence. I've been blessed.
>
> I was with soldiers in Iraq who didn't have close family ties, and they became much more emotionally attached to other soldiers. But fighting together is a different kind of relationship than having someone to talk to about what you are going through. I had friends at home I could talk to, but I didn't talk to other soldiers about my feelings. There's an unspoken rule that you don't show weakness or emotions like crying to other soldiers. We are trained to bottle them up because if you lose your cool in battle for even one second, people can get killed.

Pamela worried about how hard her son struggled with depression and anger after he left the Army and moved down to Georgia. Having members of the family nearby who could check on him helped, but she wondered how he would ever come to terms with his anger at the leaders who launched an illegal war and got so many good people on all sides of the conflict killed.

For Pamela, having a son who had to fight an illegal war in which combat entailed so much moral ambiguity carries a special responsibility. She watches out for him carefully, and, if he does not call every week, she calls him. After a war so bad, she believes it important to keep up with him and to stay close. She considers him a man with special challenges because he went to war. His reticence to talk about it does not deter her from keeping channels of conversation open and continuing to talk to him.

Both mother and son know that his life would have been very different had he not enlisted. Pamela notes:

> For the rest of my life, I will be repeating in my mind the circumstances that led up to Dweylon's enlistment in the military. I can't take back the decision to let him go. During his time in Iraq, I will always remember sleepless nights, lying in bed and wondering if my child was safe. Praying he would stay alive. Memories of that time will always haunt my life. But I am determined that what happened to him over there will not prevent my son from finding his way back to being the healthiest person he can be mentally, psychologically, and emotionally, given all he went through. I am a believer that he is going to overcome what the war did to his life.
>
> His father insists Dweylon is a grown man and does not need taking care of. But I believe he is a man with special challenges because he had to fight a war he believed was wrong. So while I agree he can take care of himself as an adult, he does need looking after because he will have to spend years processing what he did to advance an unjust war. I want to make his journey back to civilian life soft and kind after a war and nation that were not. And I believe what he has already achieved is miraculous.

Dweylon completed his undergraduate degree in psychology in May 2012 and intends to enter law school. But he feels he is several years behind where he should be, partly because his struggle with depression and motivation has slowed him down. He understands that recovery will take a long time:

It has been a difficult day-by-day process for years, but I know every year, when I look back, I have made progress. I think differently about myself and my life now than a year ago. Sometimes, when I'm sitting in class and I see students talking over the teacher or not paying attention when other students present papers, I'm amazed. In the military, you'd get a talking to for behaving that way, and I can see I learned important things in the service about discipline and respect for all kinds of people. I know I am much more aware of how people live, especially poor people in conditions that are horrible, and I got to know and talk to people who I probably would never have gotten to know otherwise because we served together. Learning so much really humbled me. I thought I knew a lot before I served, but I learned so much more.

I am more optimistic about my future and I am looking forward to my goals more than remembering the past. I know if I stay with the company of my classmates, friends, and family, I will catch up with my peers. What happened to me, the pain and memories, will never be gone from my life, but they will diminish, the more I can put one foot in front of the other and keep moving forward.

After Dweylon returned from Iraq, his best friend of twenty years, Jonathan, decided to enlist. Dweylon did his best to talk him out of it. Like him, Jonathan grew up in a military family, and his brother was already a colonel. Dweylon acknowledges that he appreciated things about military life before he went to war, just as his parents did, but he did not want his friend to go through what he had gone through, serving in what he feels was an illegal, immoral war. Finally, though, he realized that Jonathan needed to enlist for the same reasons he and others he knew in the military enlisted: they needed the income, the structure, the access to a free education, and the stability of a close-knit, disciplined community. He knew a few people who enlisted because they thought the idea of war was exciting and they wanted to fight. They were not the vast majority, however, and their need for heroics and glory made them bad soldiers who put the lives of other soldiers at risk. Thus far, Jonathan has not been deployed, but it looks as if he may be sent to Afghanistan. Dweylon stays in close touch and knows what he must do to support his friend.

KEVIN BENDERMAN WAS also supported by his close ties at home. In a short training documentary that his wife, Monica, saw, a National Guard psychiatrist, who had served in Iraq, commented about how little emotional support soldiers received in country. She remarked:

> Many of the chaplains in Iraq felt their hands were tied by the commanders of the units, just as the mental health professionals were. . . . The commanders did not want their soldiers taken out of active duty for counseling. Many commanders refused to acknowledge soldiers' questions and would not allow the chaplains the latitude to do their work.[4]

Knowing this, she sought to keep "home" as close as possible to how it was when he left. She tried to follow the same routines so, when he thought about her and what time of day it was at home, he could think about what she was doing. But when he returned, she had to move to be near his station of duty, so they worked to establish routines as much as possible.

Once their new life was established, Monica noticed Kevin's restlessness and unease. She found the Family Readiness Group program of the Army weak in the support it offered. She watched him, but rather than burden him with her concerns, she discussed them with her family. She also listened and occasionally spoke her mind, but mostly she did her best to be patient and not to push him because he had to make his own decisions. She believes holding his humanity in her heart was her most important responsibility:

> Soldiers march into hell for us. They have volunteered to defend us with their lives, and it is up to us to watch their backs. It is easy to stand on the sidelines and criticize soldiers for their actions. We, as civilians, are just as much to blame for not giving soldiers a reason to retain their humanity. We have failed in our commitment to them. If we do not change course, we have lost a great deal more than lives on a battlefield. We need to believe in the good in humanity, in the good in those who serve to defend humanity, and in our responsibility to help preserve that humanity by opposing war with peace and a real respect for all life, not only the ones we choose to acknowledge. . . . War should not be allowed to change everything.[5]

Camilo

Since he went AWOL, Camilo has continued to be very outspoken about his moral struggles with the war in Iraq. His upbringing in Roman Catholic liberation theology echoes in his frequent use of words such as *conscience, morality, values,* and *justice.* At the Truth Commission on Conscience in War hearing, Camilo heard Vietnam veteran Mac Bica speak about "moral injury," and this language connected deeply with his moral struggles.

Camilo speaks of moral injury as something that he can never leave behind: "I realized that moral injury is not something I carry with me, like a backpack I can strap to my body and drop at any time, but something that shapes an important part of who I am as a human being."[6] In his more recent writing and public speeches, Camilo explains how, in his experience, PTSD and moral injury are two different hidden wounds of war. His PTSD affects his sense of safety:

My PTSD is not very different from that of others who have been to war. . . . [In] a public place . . . I always prefer to sit with my back to the wall, . . . to see what's going on around me. I like to be in clear sight of all the exits. And I always identify places that could provide cover and concealment from possible attacks.

Camilo admits that going to therapy at the Miami VA hospital helped him to understand his trauma and how it violated his unspoken agreement of how the world should be:

That agreement stated that bombs don't explode on the road; it said that a dead cat is just that, a dead cat, and not an improvised explosive device. The agreement said that kids don't throw grenades at people, even if they're outsiders occupying their country. It said that mortar rounds don't fall from the sky as we walk to the toilet, or to the shower, or to the mess hall to eat dinner. The agreement I had with the world was that those appointed to positions of power are supposed to protect life, not to destroy it. PTSD appeared in my life when the world no longer was a safe place; when I realized I did not trust the roads anymore; when children became a mortal threat; when every beat of my heart pumped fear into my body, reminding me that my life was expendable and could be over at any moment; when death became real, and present, and graphic, and refused to leave my side, and forced me into isolation.

Camilo stresses very adamantly that his PTSD is a breach of trust with the world. Moral injury, however, is the violation of a moral agreement he had with his own internal world, his moral identity. Camilo broke that inner agreement in Iraq by violating his most deeply held moral beliefs. He fought a war that he deemed to be illegal and immoral. He allowed prisoners of war to be tortured, and he killed unarmed civilians. He also participated in the violation of a land and a civilian population. The day he killed a young man holding a grenade was a turning point in his life:

That day I knew something had forever changed inside me. I felt a hole within me that had no bottom, an infinite void that could never be replenished. For weeks after the incident, my mind could not shake off the images of the young man walking, and breathing, and then down on the ground, bloody, and dead. I once spoke with a therapist about this event. I described the incident, providing details, and explaining how I had felt and continue to feel about it. He told me that I shouldn't be so hard on myself. The young man had actually thrown a grenade that could have killed people from the crowd or, at a later time, he might have ended up killing other soldiers or civilians. I had also followed a lawful order, and I had not opened fire until I was convinced that he was indeed going to throw a grenade. I sat that day with that therapist, and on a certain level I had to agree with him. The problem was that as I observed that young man through the sight of my rifle, when he was still alive, there was something inside me, a voice one could say, that was telling me not to squeeze the trigger. And I knew, without a shred of doubt, that I should not disobey that voice, and that if I did, there would be serious consequences to face.

Camilo believes that his conscience holds a sacred universal moral law that forbids killing. Our humanity, dignity, and integrity are deeply connected to honoring our moral conscience:

When I opened fire that day, I violated that law and desecrated the most sacred sanctuary of my being. As I observed that young man through the sight of my rifle, I was staring at a point of no return, the very Rubicon of my life, and I crossed it. My moral injury is the pain I inflicted upon the very core of my being when I took something I could never give back. It is a pain that redefined my life, and that not only transformed who I was, but continues to transform me. But I don't pity myself for living with moral injury. I believe we always have a choice to take the defining moments in life, however painful they may be, and either turn them into something positive, or let them continue to destroy the core of our moral being.

Camilo admits his life was self-absorbed before he deployed to Iraq. He lived in a beautiful location and attended an expensive university. He enjoyed a vibrant intellectual life aimed at becoming a clinical psychologist and writer. He was sorry for other people's problems, but he also felt they were not his problems:

> My experience in Iraq changed that. As horrible as the experience of war was, and as painful as the memory of it continues to be, I am now a much better person than I ever was. My eyes are open and I no longer view the suffering of others as alien to my own experience. I view hunger, disease, and the brutality of war and occupation as global-scale issues, not as issues of individual nations. I believe those of us who have lived through war have a moral obligation to educate the public about what is being done in their name. But first we must recognize the fact that we have injured our moral being and core, and that repairing that damage within ourselves will require a lifelong commitment to atone for the wrongs we have committed against others.
>
> Moral injury is painful, yes, but it has also returned a sense of humanity that had been missing from my life for longer than I can remember. I have come to believe that the transformative power of moral injury cannot be found in the pursuit of our own moral balance as an end goal, but in the journey of repairing the damage we have done unto others. There is much to be learned about moral injury. . . . But if there is one thing I am certain about, it is that in committing great wrongs against others, I committed great wrongs against myself as well. And with the certainty that it will take a lifetime to heal the injuries within me, I embark on this lifelong journey to heal the injuries of others.

WHAT THESE STORIES tell us is that recovery from moral injury begins with outward expressions of an intense inner struggle. Reaching out to other veterans, family, friends, and a welcoming community may come quickly or it may come after years of silent suffering. Often, the first conversations are among veterans themselves. The emotional bonds formed in battle can be important in the transition home, and sometimes those bonds deepen into enduring friendships after the return to civilian life. As civilians, however, former comrades must come to know each other differently from the fields of battle.

In the Iraq and Afghanistan wars, over half of those who have fought come from the Reserves and National Guard, which means they return, not to military bases or large cities, but to their civilian communities where there may be few, if any, fellow veterans. They may also be too far from any VA services to use those resources. Bereft of their units and lacking other veterans who might understand their experiences of war, they struggle to rebuild their lives in isolation as aliens to the world that was once their own. In their communities, family or friends who want to understand and listen can mean the difference between a life restored and a life lost.

The arts have been for many veterans an important form of outward expression. Many programs for veterans stress the use of arts such as film, poetry, painting, and dance. Art can hold together much that is contradictory or even dangerous, placing thoughts and feelings in resonant relationships that allow for examination and reflection. Mac found in poetry a way to express his anguish as a warrior. Herm discovered how the poetry of the Psalms elicited feelings from soldiers that led to important conversations with them. Poetry touches the emotions deeply but also shapes and structures them, rather than having them erupt in raw, inchoate forms. In many ways, the act of making memories into stories requires reflection and evaluation that change our relationships to them and ourselves. Camilo and Tyler wrote their struggles and stories of Iraq as memoirs that help us understand what it is like to go to war and to return. Joshua wrote two plays about his war experiences. *Returns*, which he struggled to produce for two years, was one of nine that won a 2007 award at the National MFA Playwrights Festival: "I've created an artifact about the experience; it's something that I can engage with. . . . Getting to work with actors, put words in their mouths, that has allowed me to see things through a whole new lens. That has taken the mystery out of some of my experiences."[7]

Moral identities can be found again through friendships. Friends probe and question and challenge each other to make each other more complete. They draw out secrets and honor each other's vulnerabilities and deep longings. With friends, we discuss intimate questions, hold each other's confidences, learn to tolerate disagreements, support each other through life's struggles and joys, and explore the profound questions of life's meaning. Such friendships must include an examination of our own moral conscience in relation to what we feel and know about war.

Conversations about moral injury require deep listening. In being open, we must be willing to take in what we hear as part of ourselves, to be moved, even by what is difficult or painful to hear, and to struggle to understand profound questions about moral conscience. Hearing soul-baring truth requires resiliency to accept the worst things human beings inflict upon each other, to be present to anguish, and to let what we hear sink into us without judgment. Deep listening requires us to set our own needs aside, and to offer, simply, respect. For we reach and change others, and we ourselves are changed when we plunge to the depths of our inner life, those depths that often lie beyond articulation. Heeding those depths exposes our insecurities, our incompleteness, our need to be right and good and to make the world in our image or according to our needs.

Recovering from moral injury also requires a renewed sense of life purpose and service. A society that ends a war with a parade and returns to its entertainments, consumerism, celebrity worship, and casual commitments in order to forget its wars offers no purpose worth pursuing. To understand moral injury, we must face the cost of sending others to fight our wars and our failure to understand what it means to bring them home. Whatever we think of a war, the crucial responsibility is to accompany the journey home of those who return and remind us that, as a society, we don't just leave wars behind.

5
Soul Repair

> What does it take to kill someone?
> I mean, do you really have to squeeze
> the trigger of your rifle to kill somebody?
> DWEYLON FIFER, Iraq veteran (OIF),
> U.S. Army

> Why should we hear about body bags and deaths?
> It's not relevant. So why should I waste my
> beautiful mind on something like that?
> BARBARA BUSH, *Good Morning America*,
> March 18, 2003

The psychological and emotional effects of combat are often referred to as the "hidden wounds of war." But given veteran rates of suicide, homelessness, unemployment, divorce, depression, poverty, and imprisonment, how can such wounds really be invisible or hard to detect? Societies have many strategies for hiding the wounds of war: suppression of facts, avoidance, amnesia, and nostalgia, to name a few.

Between 1942 and 1946, John Huston directed three war documentaries. This trilogy was commissioned by the U.S. Army to celebrate the bravery of soldiers during World War II. Though the purpose of the films was clearly propaganda, Huston portrayed the complexities of war, from acts of heroism to acts of brutality. In *The Battle of San Pietro*, which took place in Southern Italy in 1943, Huston documented the killing of U.S. soldiers. He showed their body parts being bagged by their comrades and a local woman balancing a casket over her head as she walked. When the movie was first screened for the Army, several generals walked out of the room in outrage. The movie was shelved as "antiwar," and was only released later because of the direct intervention of General George Marshall, who understood its importance. *Let There Be Light*, shot in 1946, was the end of the trilogy. It followed the daily struggles of veterans in the military hospital of Mason General in Long Island. As was characteristic of the first two documentaries, Huston interviewed soldiers and let them tell their own truths. There were stories of heroism and sacrifice, which the Army certainly expected, but there were also other realities: stories of psychological trauma and images of veterans crying. Some described ambiguous feelings, including anger about the war and contempt for the military authorities. Some looked broken and anguished. One had started stuttering because of "combat fatigue." Huston also showed how military psychiatrists treated such suffering as "psychoneuroses," with methods such as hypnosis and shots of sodium amathal. The movie ended on an upbeat note by validating the positive effects of such treatment. Nonetheless, the Army refused to release *Let There Be Light*, and the movie remained unavailable until 1981. In his 1980 autobiography, *An Open Book*, Huston claimed that the army wanted the public to see only heroic warriors who remained strong, even when physically injured; it could not bear to have veterans shown in their pain and vulnerability, as broken human beings.

Today, much seems to have changed in the portrayal of war's effects on combat veterans. The public rejection of the war in Vietnam allowed for movies about the devastating cost of war, such as *The Deer Hunter* and *Full Metal Jacket*. Today, several documentaries and movies depict the tragic aftermath of the wars in Iraq and Afghanistan,

such as *The Ground Truth, Lioness, In the Valley of Elah,* and *Stop-Loss.*
If box office income and numbers of viewers are any indication, however, Americans have largely ignored such films, preferring instead to
see inspiring, entertaining, and heroic depictions of war that help us
to feel good about ourselves, to admire the behavior of soldiers, and to
deny the tragic costs of war.

After World War II, the "good" war, the country cheered battle-
weary troops, gave them parades, and welcomed them home with
open arms. After Vietnam, the "bad" war, most people turned their
backs, called the troops baby killers, or just went on with their lives as
if it hadn't happened, as if it had not dominated national attention for
years. The reactions to troops returning from Iraq have been mixed:
a "thank you for serving," some local parades, but mostly silence. Silence, perhaps, because such a small proportion of the population is
serving in the military or because people have mostly been going on
with their lives all along anyway, ignoring the wars. These are all ways
the public disposes of war and attempts to leave it behind. The silence
was encouraged by the media blackout on the images of dead soldiers
and their coffins arriving home. While the administration explained
the blackout as a form of respect for fallen soldiers, it functioned to
hide the costs and consequences of war from public consciousness.

The Afghanistan and Iraq wars enjoyed wide popular support
when they started, a fact that seems to have faded from people's
memories over the years. Debates about them as just wars fell on deaf
ears because they were launched with the language of "holy" war, as
a "crusade." On September 16, 2001, President George W. Bush declared, "This crusade, this war on terrorism is going to take a while."
The first crusade in 1095 was not a just war, but a holy pilgrimage,
an invasion to liberate Jerusalem from the Muslims, accompanied by
pogroms against Jews and internal attacks on Christians who opposed
the crusade. When the war on terror began in earnest in Afghanistan
and Iraq, a kind of national hysteria ensued. Congressional support
was nearly unanimous, though few representatives' adult children
ever served in the wars. Because France opposed the wars, Congress

banned the use of French and ate "freedom" fries, chefs poured out French wine, the Dixie Chicks had to apologize for denouncing the President and his wars, and Bill Maher and Chris Hedges got fired for opposing the conflicts. Islamophobic incidents erupted like wildfires. Only late in the summer of 2005 did public opinion turn against the war in Iraq. In August, after a monthlong antiwar occupation of Crawford, Texas, and the furious arrival and devastating aftermath of Hurricane Katrina, the polls tipped away from the Iraq War and the administration that launched it.

The "holy" wars have dragged on well beyond the capacity of the public to remember the heady patriotic days of their popularity. Regardless of popular opinion or its lack, however, a war does not end when the troops return. It simply comes home and embeds itself in civilian life. Veterans face a return to a society obsessed with political posturing and polarized debates. The public has, thus far, demonstrated scant willingness to fund veteran recovery, and discussions are few about our moral responsibility for sending others to fight a war in our name. Even fewer citizens seek to know or hear what war has done to our own people or to other countries.

Most civilian actions toward veterans shield us from accepting our own complicity in war. Who needs veterans to "put the war behind you and move on with your life" and who benefits from the suppression of veteran suffering? Mac Bica observes:

> Veterans [must] confront and then work through the enormity of the experience of war, the trauma, and the moral realization that they have participated in an enterprise whose only purpose is to kill and mutilate other human beings for a cause that is, at best, legally and morally questionable and ambiguous. . . . So, appreciating and thanking a veteran for her "service," calling her a hero, is counterproductive, as it creates a distraction from the difficult task of confronting the moral enormity of the enterprise of war. That is, it provides a sanctuary of sorts—a safe haven—the mythology to which she may escape when the healing journey gets

tough and threatening—and it will—as it is much preferable and comfortable to think oneself a hero, flawed though we may be, than a murderer and a dupe. Besides, all such gestures of respect and appreciation are, in reality, a charade, insincere, pseudo-patriotic talk intended to hype sales at the mall and to entice other naive young people to believe war is glorious and heroic, luring them into military service to become the tools and cannon fodder of future wars for profit and power.

Unfortunately, healing and coming home from war are difficult, complex, and perilous journeys of introspection and understanding. So, while it is important that veterans not be ostracized, shunned, or ignored should they want to talk, if healing is to occur, it must be with the help of others who have shared the experience, who know the horror firsthand. We are not helped through telling war stories to well-intentioned but voyeuristic civilians. . . . Our healing does not require civilian understanding, sympathy, or compassion, nor is healing enhanced by civilian appreciation, respect, and admiration.

As every story in this book makes clear, veterans need the love, respect, and support of friends and family who know them personally and who will accompany them on the long struggle to recover from war. Pamela has continued to study and teach about war in the years since Dweylon has been home. She has reflected, especially, on a society's relationship to war:

The more I research, the more I am convinced that a large component of military personnel are in the military for financial survival. We have got to draw deeper connections about poor people being recruited into the military to fight rich men's wars. I've reexamined Martin Luther King's sermon from April 4, 1967, "Beyond Vietnam: A Time to Break Silence," and I have marveled at his sensitivity to issues of class and race with regard to war. I have found, over and over, that a good number of soldiers also grasp these issues. They understand that for many of our contemporary wars, they are not over there for our or another nation's self-defense. They are sent into many war zones to protect the interests of the wealthy and powerful. The hypocrisy that costs our soldiers is bad enough, but it is tragic that the majority who suffer in wars we initiate and execute are noncombatant women and children. They suffer the most. They are killed, or raped and impoverished; their countries are wrecked, and their lives are destroyed. Looking at my son and what it cost him to be at war, I know it was wrong. I have watched his journey to reintegrate. I've watched Dweylon struggle to become a civilian after all he went through, and I pray for him and all the others.

It is easier to take a clear, unambiguous position against all wars if one has the resources and family support to avoid or leave military service. If our society provided a living wage in any job, affordable housing, free universal health care, and high-quality education through college, it is not clear how many young people would still volunteer for military service, but the struggle of combat veterans to receive adequate treatments and be restored to civilian life would be greatly eased.

For every soldier, the choice to fight or to refuse to fight carries serious, lifelong consequences. As is evident in reflections from Herm, Dweylon, and Camilo, the opportunity to fight in war is not a reason many men and women join the military. Instead, their motives are often quite mixed and complex. Whatever their individual motives for joining the armed services, all men and women not only are trained to fight, but are also taught the moral conduct of war. When soldiers morally oppose a war, they have to weigh their personal feelings against loyalty to their unit and comrades, as well as to consider the consequences of refusing a direct order..

In an attempt to mitigate the impact of war on soldiers, the Department of Defense developed a Comprehensive Soldier Fitness (CSF) program in 2009 with an investment of at least $125 million. The program assesses fitness for war in five different areas: physical, emotional, social, familial, and spiritual, with the goal of enhancing strength in all areas. The definition for "spiritual fitness" is vaguely stated as "[s]trengthening a set of beliefs, principles or values that sustain a person beyond family, institutional, and societal sources of strength."[1]

The meaning of spiritual strength, however, fails to contain any moral content or to acknowledge the basic existence of moral conscience, which is the key to distinguishing a healthy person from a sociopath. Instead, it seems to rely on individual capacities to think positively. It defines the spiritually fit as:

> better able to accept the reality of a situation, develop creative coping strategies, find meaning in trauma, maintain an optimistic view of the future, access their social support network, generate the motivation to persevere, grow from adversity, and mitigate serious psychological problems such as posttraumatic stress disorder. . . . Individuals who report stronger spiritual motivation also manifest less conflict among other goals in their lives, greater purpose in life, greater commitment to their goals, and more satisfaction and happiness in the pursuit of their strivings.[2]

The idea of cultivating military spiritual fitness is not new. In 1987, the Army distributed a fifteen-page pamphlet, "Spiritual Fitness," that opened with a quote by General G. C. Marshall: "The soldier's heart, the soldier's spirit, the soldier's soul are everything." The pamphlet stresses the importance of cultivating the kind of spirit that will lead to victory. However, some sections of the 1987 document also mention the negative side of war:

> b. Members of Health Services Command and the Chaplain Corps continue to address the issues of suicide prevention, stress management, and battle fatigue. Techniques for implementing these emotional fitness areas are included in the Stress Management Module.

c. Spiritual well-being is important since soldiers function more effectively when they have a support system or framework of meaning to sustain them. However, spiritual fitness is little talked about by most soldiers nor is it planned for in unit training. Yet, we constantly deal with the soldier's spirit. It is the quality of the soldier's spirit which translates the professional Army ethic into realistic expectations for the way we do business.

d. Spiritual fitness is the development of those personal quali-ties needed to sustain a person in times of stress, hardship, and tragedy. These qualities come from religious, philosophical, or hu-man values and form the basis for character, disposition, decision making, and integrity.

e. This definition presupposes that visible action stems from our spiritual health and comes from our set of values.[3]

Despite this material, the rising suicide and PTSD rates among active-duty military and veterans of Afghanistan and Iraq in the past decade have been alarming. Army suicides have increased steadily since 2004, and the new 2009 Spiritual Fitness section of the CSF program seems to be a response, especially to the loss of a sense of purpose as the wars have ground on for a decade without a clear goal or measurable end. The 2009 program notes:

The Army needs resilient members of the Army community. Re-silience, or the ability to bounce back from stress and trauma, has been a hallmark of the American Soldier for more than two cen-turies. Nevertheless, we cannot ignore the fact that our Army has been at war for nearly a decade, that many members of our commu-nity have multiple combat deployments, and these deployments have not only taken a toll on Soldiers, but have also taken a toll on the Family members left behind and the Department of the Army Civilians who support them in theater and at home. We are committed to a true prevention model, aimed at the entire force, which will enhance resilience and coping skills enabling them to grow and thrive in today's Army.[4]

One assumption of the 2009 Spiritual Fitness material is that a soldier who is more deeply able to understand the deep interconnectedness of beings would be more willing to sacrifice self for a deeper purpose or for love of another. Brigadier General Rhonda Cornum, director of CSF, remarked that spiritual people make better soldiers because of "the ethos [they] adhere to: Always place the mission first. Never accept defeat. Never leave a fallen comrade—Those kinds of things require you to have a belief in something higher than yourself."[5]

General Cornum's comment leaves out what is also a striking absence in the literature on spiritual fitness in the military: the role of moral conscience in spirituality and empathy for others beyond the confines of battle comrades. In the face of the moral struggles of combat veterans we have witnessed, the spiritual fitness dimension of CSF is strikingly unconcerned about the deep moral questions posed by war, and it seems to glorify soldiers as spiritually fit who can remain unaffected in any deep moral or emotional way. Basic training seems to reinforce this amoral perspective. Chas Davis, a soldier who became a CO, was appalled by having to sing "Sniper Wonderland" as part of military drill:

> See the little girl with the puppy;
> Lock and load a hollow pointed round . . .
> Take the shot and maybe if you're lucky;
> You'll watch their lifeless bodies hit the ground . . .
> Through the fields we'll be walkin';
> 'Cross the rooftops we'll be stalkin' . . .
> One shot one kill from the top of the hill . . .
> Walkin' in a sniper wonderland.[6]

An amoral approach to spiritual fitness stigmatizes veterans with moral injury as spiritually "unfit." It also attempts to make the injuries of war into something positive. In a widely syndicated story in the *New York Times*, the Army's CSF ten-day Master Resilience Training Program offered examples of the "positive value" of PTSD. Spirituality and resilience were depicted as a form of positive thinking achieved through exercises such as asking soldiers to practice seeing events in a neutral light instead of labeling them as good or bad. Another exercise involves creating a nightly list of the positive things that happened during that day, in order to learn to focus on the positive. At no point was there any indication of what it might mean to ask someone to think of an atrocity or other act that violates either moral conscience or the military code of honor as a neutral or positive act. How is something like "Sniper Wonderland" or killing unarmed civilians morally neutral?[7]

The spiritual fitness and resilience training aspects of CSF completely bypasses the difficult ethical questions that healthy human beings ask after participating in war. Once again, veterans who struggle with their emotions and ask moral questions after war are stigmatized as having a personal weakness that needs "fixing" to achieve greater spiritual fitness. We, on the other hand, cannot imagine spiritual "fitness" without moral conscience. In religious and moral traditions, moral conscience defines soul not just for the individual but for the whole community. Such conscience is grounded in empathy and compassion for others and the capacity to recognize what is good and to know when something is profoundly wrong. That so many veterans manage to hold on to moral conscience in the face of so much pressure to suppress it, and suffer to the point of suicide rather than abandon their souls, is testimony to the resilience of conscience and to their basic goodness.

When a community takes responsibility for helping those with moral injury, it must do so with integrity, rather than by scapegoating individuals or pressuring them to deny what they know to be true. Both an insistence on positive thinking and the punishing of individuals fail to address the morally compromising nature of war. Positive thinking denies moral truth, and inflicting harsh judgment on those who understand their moral transgressions in war deepens the inner condemnations of conscience and steals the will to live.

At the same time, we must also be careful about the use of forgiveness. In wanting to overcome the pain of moral self-condemnations, we can be tempted to want to offer forgiveness too quickly—these are the safe havens of parades, thank-yous, and expressions of admiration that Mac rejects. And when someone who was not injured by war offers forgiveness, it can be a way to protect the forgiver from having to understand moral injury and a society from having to face the unalterable tragedies of war.

Premature forgiveness may be cathartic and offer emotional relief, but receiving such forgiveness requires amnesia about the full extent of harm that war inflicts. Facile forgiveness interferes with veterans facing the truth of what they did. It may offer anesthesia for the pain of moral injury, but premature forgiveness can create an addiction to relief, and it can reinforce a need to tell horror stories, enact guilt, and solicit forgiveness. This cycle relieves moral responsibility temporarily instead of building the lifelong strength to live with it. Without the ability to remember what violated moral conscience, moral identity cannot be rebuilt, either in an individual or in a society that refuses its own responsibility for war.

One form of collective false forgiveness is what anthropologist Renato Rosaldo calls "imperialist nostalgia," a profound yearning for a romantic view of the past destroyed by war, which is the corollary to war's demonization of the enemy. When imperial powers wage war against opponents, they must first demonize their enemy, using racist stereotypes to stir up fear and hatred. These stereotypes are not images of real, complex human beings but a slurry from which an army constructs its own power and authorization for violence. To stir up such hostility against an imaginary "other" can, however, have devastating unintended consequences. Demonizing one group within a multicultural military challenges the unit cohesion required in combat. For example, as Islamophobia was used for a "crusade against terrorism," American Muslims serving in the armed forces became targets of hate crimes. They were also required to violate an Islamic prohibition against killing other Muslims. In June 2004, when Sergeant 1st Class Abdullah Webster was jailed for refusing to deploy to Iraq, Captain Hamza Al-Mubarak, an Air Force chaplain, testified on his behalf.

The demonization and hate stirred up for war are not restricted to military training. For a public to support a war against an enemy, we too must accept the dehumanization of other countries and their people. Demonization has serious consequences in the long, lingering aftermath of war. Once the enemy is defeated, the emotional, nationalistic bonds of hate built on imaginary slurs and fused by war gradually lose their usefulness, and the hollowed imagination of the conqueror needs new content upon which to construct itself as noble and good. The vanquished enemy, now no longer to be feared, often becomes an object of admiration and a projection of the conquerors' need to be restored to goodness. Rosaldo writes:

> A person kills somebody and mourns the victim. In more attenuated form, someone deliberately alters a form of life, and then regrets that things have not remained as they were prior to the intervention. At one more remove, people destroy their environment, and then they worship nature. In any of its versions, imperialist nostalgia uses a pose of "innocent yearning" both to capture people's imaginations and to conceal its complicity with often brutal domination.[8]

Imperialist nostalgia can inspire people to adopt vanquished cultural forms and religions, which are recycled from slurry into romantic stereotypes. In attempting wistfully to reincarnate what they imagine they have destroyed but of which they still lack any deep knowledge, victors may also seek forgiveness, absolution, and friendship with survivors or descendants among their former enemies. Absolution keeps the imperialist of the present at the center of the drama about forgiveness for the past. In drawing its emotional power from nostalgia, absolution denies economic, racial, linguistic, and national power differences and the devastations of war that continue in the present— in effect, using greater power to demand that those who have been harmed assuage the guilt of their conquerors. Imperialists maintain false innocence through solicitous kindness, paternalistic charity, admiration for the imaginary other, and the "elegance of manners." In doing so, they maintain their own privilege and fail to make themselves vulnerable to engaged, complex, and intimate relationships that challenge the imperialist script.[9]

A blatant example of such an imperialist script is the 1990s musical *Miss Saigon*, an adaptation of the "Madame Butterfly" story to the Vietnam War era, what people in Vietnam call the "American war." It tells the story of a native woman who loves an imperialist cad because he is better than any native man, forcing her to sacrifice all for his world. Miss Saigon is a young, orphaned Vietnamese prostitute, Kim, who is pledged in marriage to an evil North Vietnamese man, Thuy. She falls in love with an American Marine, Chris, who pledges to save her. But the Marine leaves and marries an American woman, while Kim, who has his son, goes into hiding and waits for him. When Thuy finds Kim, he tries to kill the boy, forcing Kim to shoot him with his own gun. Kim's pimp sees the American boy as a ticket out and moves with Kim and her son to Bangkok. Chris learns about them, and after confessing to his American wife, he travels to Bangkok. Since the imperialist is the heart of the story, Kim, with no possibility of a future in her own land, has to kill herself so Chris and his American wife can take her son away to a better life.

When the imperialist is not the focus of the drama, it loses its nostalgic power. The cross-dressing Asian male character in David Henry Hwang's play *M. Butterfly*, based on a true story, comments on the silliness of this imperialist trope to a clueless French diplomat, who is in love with the ideal "oriental" woman performed by the Asian man. The Asian man highlights the ludicrous nature of the imperialist dream of love by turning it into the story of a blonde homecoming queen who falls in love with an Asian businessman who leaves her. She chooses to wait for his return while refusing a proposal from a Kennedy. Eventually, she has to kill herself so their son can have a better life in Asia with her lover's Asian wife.

Imperialist nostalgia underlies one strategy some therapists have tried with Vietnam veterans. They take veterans back to Vietnam to conduct service projects to atone for their feelings of guilt. The veterans visit religious services, offer gifts, and ask forgiveness of descendants of the war. Such acts are supposed to help veterans "make peace with themselves, rehumanize, and reconcile with the other, and restore the broken world order."[10] This strategy may alleviate guilt, but it is an imperialist atonement that costs the former imperialists very little, as is evident from the description of such practices. Rather than learning to speak the language, forming serious relationships with Vietnamese human beings as individuals, and sharing their living conditions over an extended period of time, the veterans interact with the Vietnamese as objectified symbols of American veterans' redemption. The imperialist economic world order remains intact.

One such imperialist story of "atonement" illustrates how the symbolic objectification of human beings persists after such token gestures of atonement are accomplished. An American veteran on one of these atonement trips bought a water buffalo and a calf for a farmer as an atoning act because the unnamed farmer lived in an area where the vet had killed many such animals. The veteran asked the local peasants to forgive him, and the recipient of the gifts blessed him, told him to forgive himself, and asked him to return as his cousin. The veteran's second trip illustrates how the drama was about his own redemption, not a respectful, responsible relationship to real people. The therapist describes with approval that on that second trip, the veteran and others "wandered Viet Nam's streets, practicing 'random acts of kindness' with huge smiles as they distributed American dollar bills to any poor people they met."[11] Since relationships with real human beings were not at issue, "poor people" can function as targets of largesse to help the imperialist feel good, just as in the past the demonized ancestors of the poor "other" were targets of bullets and bombs. This is a very expensive way to buy cheap forgiveness.

People subject to imperialist nostalgia may choose to participate in the drama of forgiveness and absolution for a variety of reasons. In blessing the veteran and telling him to forgive himself, the Vietnamese farmer may have been indicating that he was not interested in playing a role in the imperialist's drama and chose to maintain his freedom to be kind and hospitable to a stranger. Forgiveness may be offered as a protective strategy for preventing further harm or for maximizing the flow of charity, especially financial resources. Forgiveness is an act of personal agency, which means it can be a decision to reject a victim identity of helplessness and to use one's power to sever bonds of trauma so the imperialist no longer dominates the story. In effect, forgiveness can be a way to ignore the imperialist racist slurry and its recycled admired victim. In deciding that perpetrators of war will no longer be able to control their feelings or dominate their thoughts and memories of the traumatic past, survivors choose a future free of what perpetrators want or feel. They may also actually care about the perpetrators, though an offer of forgiveness may simply be a compassionate act of assuaging pain, since someone who did not directly suffer harm also cannot forgive it.

The hidden ghosts of war haunt the imperialist drama. The vanquished dead cannot forgive, and survivors cannot forgive on behalf of the dead. When the living refuse to perform their nostalgic role as noble people and, instead, challenge their conquerors to be morally accountable for the harm they caused, the imperialist can easily turn hostile and revert to demonization. The noble drama is far easier to enact when the vanquished live in a deeply impoverished and decimated distant land, where, once the drama is enacted, the players do not have to shape a just society where an honest life together in the present might become possible.

Veterans who return from a war with moral injury are both the imperialist and the vanquished. They leave behind their moral failures inscribed on the bodies, cities, and soil of the conquered, and they bring those horrors home in their souls. They also return to a nation that, thus far, has proved unwilling or unable to accept responsibility for sending them to war, preferring instead to project their own dramas upon veterans as noble heroes, traumatized victims, or baby killers who just need individual therapy. In refusing to play their part in these dramas, veterans who challenge the society to engage in a deeper moral discernment process offer ways to stop the imperialist drama and face the deeper costs of war.

Herm retired at the rank of colonel with forty-five decorations, including a Purple Heart. He has made the protection of moral conscience his life's work. From 1992 to 1994, he was invited to work at the Department of Defense, and he almost succeeded in changing conscientious objection to include just war ideas. He retired in 1998 but was called back to work for the secretary of the Army, and in 2000, he was asked to remain on active duty to work at the State Department for the Ambassador at Large for International Religious Freedom. Herm continues in retirement to work on protecting the moral consciences of soldiers sent to wars they believe are illegal and immoral. In addition, he has turned his attention to religious communities and their failure to do enough for veterans.

> I want my religious community to see this new work on moral injury as a challenge to make a "place of grace" for our veterans. I feel both sad and mad when I hear church leaders say, "Our church does not have these people coming to see us. If they stay away, we have no opportunity to help them."
>
> The religious community that does nothing but wait will be of no help for the veterans returning from the war. I ask, "What happened to 'Go into all the world . . . '" We must invite and welcome strangers into our community and help them feel at home.

What does it mean for religious communities to create a "place for grace," a place to recover from moral injury? Moral conscience and a moral identity require empathy, a capacity to see others as human beings with their own feelings and needs. "Going out into all the world" would require cultivating such empathy not only toward veterans but also to everyone harmed by war, and accepting moral responsibility for our role in such harm. To be a reliable space for recovery requires this courage, honesty, and humility in order to hear, acknowledge, and be accountable for the complex truths about war and all that leads to it.

An intense, ritualized community process called basic training takes a group of ordinary people and toughens them into a combat unit. As Mac explained when recounting his training in chapter 2, this process is designed to break down the natural reluctance to killing that most human beings share. For many soldiers forced to chant, "Kill, kill, kill! Kill without mercy," and trained in reflexive shooting, moral injury begins during basic training. In fact, we have met a few women who applied for CO status right after boot camp because they realized their moral core was being assaulted and that such killing was impossible for them to do. What does it mean to belong to a society that asks human beings to surrender their moral agency for war? To engage veterans with integrity means we must acknowledge that the atrocities of war are not exceptions or aberrations to a moral norm. Rather, they are part of the nature of war itself, even of "just" wars and "good" wars. As Mac insists:

> Life amid the violence, death, horror, trauma, anxiety, and fatigue of war erodes moral being, undoes character, and reduces decent men and women to savages capable of incredible cruelty that would never have been possible before their having been victimized by and sacrificed to war. As evidenced by the appalling events in Haditha and Baghdad and so many others—including the recent atrocity committed when several Marines urinated on the lifeless bodies of Taliban fighters—warriors are dehumanized and desensitized to death and destruction. Judgments of right and wrong—morality—quickly become irrelevant, and cruelty and brutality become a primal response to an overwhelming threat of annihilation. Consequently, atrocities in such an environment are not isolated, aberrant occurrences prosecuted by a few deviant individuals. Rather, they are commonplace, intrinsic to the nature and the reality of war, the inevitable consequence of enduring prolonged, life-threatening, and morally untenable conditions, what psychologist Robert Jay Lifton describes as "atrocity-producing situations."[12]

To engage veterans' moral struggles without recognizing our society's responsibilities for war is disingenuous, self-serving, and ultimately futile. Joshua Casteel raises the question of social responsibility in *Soldiers of Conscience*, when he reflects on a comment that haunted him: "We sleep comfortably in our beds at night because violent men do violence on our behalf." Referring to that quote, he says, "When I first read that, I thought to myself, I am the person who allows people to sleep comfortably in their beds at night." After gaining conscientious objector status in 2005, he began to think about why a so-called peaceful society relies on war for its security, and what it means to train ordinary young people to be killers. He traveled around the country speaking about his conversion from war with Christian Peacemaker Teams, an organization of people who volunteer to live in war zones as peacemakers.

The fact that many veterans live in anguish because of moral injury while most citizens still sleep comfortably at night is not evidence of a collective clean conscience. It is evidence of a lack of awareness and accountability. We cannot uphold our moral integrity by pleading an ignorance of facts, by claiming a war is legal, or by distancing ourselves from the leaders who declare a war. To treat veterans with respect means to examine our collective relationship to war with the same standards of courage and integrity veterans themselves have modeled.

The story of Kevin Benderman is one example of such courage and integrity. Kevin understood his decision to refuse to redeploy as upholding the honor and integrity of military service, which taught him to respect the truth. In choosing a career in the military, he swore to defend his country, not, as he states, "to invade another country, steal its resources, and destroy the lives of its people." The forty-year-old soldier was horrified by the atrocities against Iraqi civilians committed by U.S. soldiers. He grieved for what he saw war do to all affected by it. He took personal responsibility for learning about the Iraqi people by speaking with them and by reading their holy book, a commitment that deepened his moral injury as he understood more clearly their humanity and how he was like them.

His wife, Monica, challenged the verdict against him:

The Army has removed itself so completely from its moral responsibility, that its representatives are willing to openly demand, in a court of law, that they be allowed to regain "positive control over this soldier" by finding him guilty of crimes he did not commit, and put him in jail—a prisoner of conscience, for daring to obey a moral law. . . . It is "hard work" to face the truth, and it is scary when people who are not afraid to face it begin to speak out. Someone once said that my husband's case is a question of morality over legality. I pray that this country has not gone so far over the edge that the two are so distinctly different that we can tell them apart.[13]

In the wake of being punished for speaking out about the "madness of war," Kevin has spent a great deal of time educating himself about the politics of wars, the corporations that profit from them, and the legal violations of the authorities who launch them. Kevin believes that "protest demonstrations to stop wars are useless. People are still driven by their fears to believe propaganda rather than to challenge the lies that send people to war. I'd like to see demonstrations to demand prosecution of the people who launched the wars." He believes the public trusts too much in truth to fix the problem of war. Information about what it does to people and countries is not hidden, but the many news stories, books, and documentaries about current and past wars seem to have done little to prevent war.

Kevin believes the public distances itself from moral responsibility for war and denies justice to all those killed in illegal or immoral wars by failing to prosecute and hold accountable those who launch such wars: "I hate it when folks call people in the military 'the troops,' like we aren't human or something. That kind of label takes away who you are as human beings, like we aren't part of humanity and like we don't deserve justice from people who sent us into an immoral war." He is clear that people in the military "start out as civilians, just like everybody else, and we go back to civilian life." But the civilian public has failed to "demand justice for those who fought and those who died." He observes that after World War II, the German public was condemned for failing to resist Nazi rule, even though information was available from early on about its crimes. It is commonplace in the United States to criticize the German society of that time, but Kevin challenges this stance as hypocritical: "The American public should not criticize the Germans; what has it done instead? It has failed to take responsibility for Iraq." Lies about weapons of mass destruction and the failure to link Saddam Hussein to Al Qaeda emerged within months of the invasion of Iraq, but as the rationale for war shifted to helping the Iraqi people, the fighting ground on for a decade. Until the public demands an accounting, Kevin is certain that the country's leaders, trusting in military power, mesmerized by weapons systems, and oblivious to the cost of war on ordinary people, will fail to use intelligence, moral reasoning, and common sense in dealing with international problems.

What would it mean to claim our personal and collective moral integrity? It means understanding that some wounds of war, such as PTSD, require treatment, but it is not just an individual diagnosis. It is part of a larger social consequence of war and, therefore, not simply a private problem that can be solved by therapy. To address it requires engaging moral questions about decisions to go to war with families, communities, and society.

When such dialogues occur, they mine a deeper level of moral questioning in which language moves from being descriptive to being deeply transformative. Speaking about moral injury places morality, justice, and human dignity at the center of public attention and exposes a collective amnesia about war, its victims, and its aftermath. To listen to the witnesses of veterans who struggle with moral injury shifts the conversation from the individual issues of some soldiers after the war to larger questions about war. Camilo argues that he speaks out about his life so that civilians can somehow experience the war though his eyes and see it with greater complexity. This includes helping U.S. citizens to consider the effects of war and occupation on the "enemy," one of Camilo's most pressing concerns: "We want regular civilians to know about the suffering of Iraqis, and how our military operations are carried out in the countries we occupy."[14]

The veterans who speak about their moral injury and the cost of the latest wars on U.S. soldiers do so with a deep concern for the people they fought against. They are not asking for public interest in U.S. veterans that would disregard the realities and the humanity of Iraqi and Afghani people. Tyler is adamant about this:

It's always about *the troops*. But "moral injury" by definition includes the memories of those who have been harmed. Without the Iraqi people, the troops can have no moral injury to speak of. And the only way Americans can fathom the meaning of this term, "moral injury," is to acknowledge the humanity of the Iraqis. The two ideas are inseparable. . . .

Moral injury is a term that loosens the noose a bit around the necks of veterans who are harangued by enormous personal guilt and distributes the responsibility for their actions (justified or not) more evenly around the chain of command, the government, and maybe even the American people. Simultaneously, moral injury reaches out to those who may be too quick to exculpate themselves. It broadens the burden of responsibility for acts that may not be criminal by the strict sense of the law but that are clearly hurtful to other people and, therefore, morally questionable. It implicates all participants of war, whether commanding, supporting, or just standing idly by, and it gives a name from the hurt that comes from doing so.[15]

While civilians and veterans may both experience moral injury, we would be disingenuous if we claimed that each experiences the same moral anguish. When Camilo and Gabriella discussed this very issue, Camilo remarked, "Yes, you and I share responsibility for the war. Society at large does. But I killed a human being. I can never take that back. I can never undo it. I can never forget it." Equating our collective responsibility with the moral anguish of soldiers trivializes the struggles of veterans. Similarly, acknowledging moral injury as a society does not give U.S. civilians license to claim the status of "victims."

Holocaust survivor Primo Levi was outraged at how easily perpetrators of violence came to be portrayed as victims themselves over time. In his last book, *The Drowned and the Saved*, he urged society not to commit this mistake of adding insult to the horrors already suffered by victims of violence. While he does not deny that the tendency to commit violence may lie in all humans, in many contexts, the difference between innocent victims and victimizers is not ambiguous. Levi wrote:

> I do know that I was guiltless victim and I was not a murderer. I know that the murderers existed, not only in Germany, and still exist retired or on active duty, and that to confuse them with their victim is a moral disease or an aesthetic affectation or a sinister sign of complicity; above all, it is precious service rendered (intentionally or not) to the negators of truth.[16]

The veterans in this book are very clear about the complexity of their moral positions and do not indulge in the easy and self-indulgent stance of slipping into a victim role. They remain fiercely committed to avoiding denial and forgetting. They seek to remember what they did personally to harm others and to take responsibility for how they violated their own moral conscience as their route to recovery.

Engaging in collective conversations about moral injury and war can help us all to strengthen the moral fabric of society and the connections that tie us to the rest of the world. Our collective engagement with moral injury will teach us more about the impact of our actions and choices on each other, enable us to see the world from other perspectives, and chart pathways for our future. If we achieve deeper and more open ways to grasp the complexities of human relationships, we will be able to understand power and the vast and complex ways we can misuse our power.

We cannot turn the clock back to prewar times; we cannot bring back the dead, or undo atrocities and environmental destruction. We must resist offering hasty forgiveness to absolve ourselves and others. If we can take the time, instead, to listen to what veterans say to us, to befriend them as we journey together toward a different world, we can together discover how deep transformation leads us toward the moral conscience that is the deepest, most important dimension of our shared humanity. In doing so, we can come to understand the honor and integrity of military service and the importance of the moral criteria for war, which the military itself teaches, and what it would require of every one of us to send any one of us to war.

Soul repair is how we hold on to our own humanity and how, at the same time, we can face the unbearable truths of who we can be in war. It requires us to engage the difficult truths of war and our relationship to it, a process that is at once both individual and collective. It is about "remembering" the truth of what we did and who we are, so that we might reweave our moral fiber as people and as a nation.

In accepting our moral responsibility for the many devastations of war, we may begin an honest reassessment and renewal of our relationship to our own humanity, to each other, to the rest of the world, and to all that sustains life. We come to know another way to live is possible. In *Soldiers of Conscience*, Joshua Casteel affirmed, "I have a different picture of tomorrow's humanity and I want to be involved in creating that."

Conclusion

When we began our work on moral injury in 2009, we found a way to understand both the veterans in our families and the men and women who have become our friends through our work on the Truth Commission. Veterans who appear in this book, as well as many others we have met during talks on moral injury, have challenged us to think more carefully about the moral complexities of military service and about civilian responsibility for reintegrating veterans into our society. The process of working with veterans on their struggles with their conscience and with moral injury profoundly changed how we feel and think about soldiers and how we approach moral issues of war and peace.

Through the process of listening, we have become less absolute in our personal opposition to war, and we have come to understand how moral conscience is deeply important for those who choose military service. Because of the humanity of those who serve, we believe a society must never rush to war, but challenge its leaders to explain why it is the only alternative. And through our friendship with veterans of war who so generously helped us with this book, we have come to understand our own lives differently.

Gabriella

One early morning in June 2009, I was reading the Italian news on *Repubblica Online* when a simple headline on a sidebar caught my attention. Clicking on the link, I found a story about the southern city of Trani, Puglia, a town of fifty-five thousand people. A young veteran had attacked his mother with a knife and then killed himself. No names were mentioned. Though my cousin Giuseppe and my aunt Nietta lived in Trani, I had no reason to think the story was about them. Yet, as soon as I read the headline, I "knew." I searched for additional details, which were just emerging: the unnamed veteran had been on leave for depression and unspecified mental issues and was living with his mother, a retired nurse. They lived in a storefront apartment. The thirty-year-old man, who apparently had never given signs of violent behavior before, had stabbed his mother fifteen times. The sixty-six-year-old woman, left for dead by the son, managed to crawl to the door and under the shutter to the street outside, crying out for help. The first thing she asked her rescuers was to help her son first.

Had I not worked closely with veterans and learned that PTSD and moral injury can lead to terrible tragedies in any family, I would not have made the connection so quickly, but the details in the news were eerily familiar. My aunt had been a nurse and she lived for a long time in a storefront apartment. I called my sister in Italy and I begged her to call my uncle Angelo to check on my intuition. When she did so, my uncle had just received a notification call from the police. He learned that my aunt Nietta was still alive but in critical condition. The first thing she asked when she regained consciousness was if her son was still alive.

I was living in California, but I understood that the headline in *Repubblica* was about us before my family in Italy received the news—even before the police were able to notify the next of kin. I was grateful that my father had not lived to witness that day. When he had passed away two years earlier, his sister in Trani had not traveled to Turin for the funeral. Her excuse was that her son Giuseppe was not well emotionally and she could not leave him alone. My sister and I were a bit hurt by our aunt's decision. Couldn't he be left alone for a couple of days, we wondered? And why couldn't he travel to the funeral himself? After all, my father had been very kind to him through the years. We thought they were just coming up with excuses, and we could not understand their absence.

I had a similar reaction when Giuseppe decided to stay in the army after completing his year of conscription. I was surprised, since I knew he was not enthusiastic about military service. I attributed it to economic pressures and the high unemployment rate, but still, I thought, he could have made a better choice if he only tried harder. My father distrusted the military and was upset by his nephew's choice; I was similarly distressed by it. I grew up in a post–World War II culture that feared the Cold War could end in nuclear annihilation. As part of my Waldensian church youth group, I trained as a peace educator and offered free workshops on nonviolent transformation of conflicts. When most of my male friends faced a year of conscription after they turned eighteen, they applied for conscientious objector status, which required a rather punitive two-year program of community service. I admired them. While as a young woman, I did not have to face the draft, I was judgmental about people like my cousin who did not take a stronger stance for a culture of peace. Today, after having listened to so many veterans' stories about the complex reasons they joined the army, I am able to see my cousin's choice differently. Some people join the military because they feel they have no alternatives. I think this was my cousin's situation.

Giuseppe was born and raised in Puglia, in the South, whereas I grew up in the more affluent northern part of Italy. My father traveled to the North from Puglia when he was a teenager, along with millions of others seeking a better life. When Italy was "reconstructed" after World War II, the North was the main focus of development, but those who migrated to the factories of Milan or Turin were treated like second-class citizens. While Giuseppe and I came from the same economic background, we had access to very different public services and to different life options. My sister and I were the first in our family to go to college and graduate school; Giuseppe and his brother only completed high school. My rather patronizing attitude about Giuseppe's choice to join the military was to think my cousin did not have adequate critical tools to realize how misguided his choice was. Years later, when he was sent on "peacekeeping" missions around the world, I was more worried for the people at the receiving end of the Italian help than for those who delivered it. I did not try to understand what going to war zones might have meant for him.

In the days following Giuseppe's death, most papers reported the story using almost the same words. A few defined the attempted murder and suicide as "a tragedy caused by loneliness and social malaise." No one linked it to the fact that my cousin had been sent on multiple "peace missions" abroad or commented that such peace missions are an Orwellian euphemism for going to war, since the Italian Constitution forbids any war unless Italy is directly attacked.

On that tragic day in June two years ago, I had been immersed in my work with the Truth Commission on Conscience in War and moral injury. After hearing so many stories from veterans and their families, I was shocked by the news, but I could also make some sense of it. Earlier in my life, I might have felt ashamed that my family was in the newspaper as a "classic" example of the sad life of the poor and socially maladjusted: seminary professors and ministers usually are not associated with grisly murders and hand-wringing in the national press. But I knew those news commentaries were no more than convenient explanations that hid the complex truth about Italian "peace missions" and the outrageous lack of proper mental health care for Italian veterans. I read the story, not as an isolated case of madness, but as part of a larger and pressing problem involving veterans and their families. I passed the news articles around to my closest friends and colleagues, both in Italy and the United States, to make them more aware of veterans' issues. I also realized that speaking about the cost of war was not only about my family's past, but still about my very present. I was never speaking and writing about "them," but always also about "us," even when I did not fully know it.

In the spring of 2011, when my mother called to say that my uncle Albert shot himself at age eighty-eight, I was deeply grieved and yet not totally surprised. By then, I had a deeper understanding about the lifetime of anguish suffered by many people who have experienced war and atrocities. I had often felt that after coming back from Mauthausen, my uncle had been tormented, even if he hid it very well. He became an aggressively successful businessman, he vacationed around the world, and he maintained close ties with his friends from the Resistance who were still alive. He always seemed to have a very close relationship with his wife, a remarkably beautiful woman even as she aged. She was the one who found him still barely breathing in a pool of blood.

I confess that while I admired my uncle's moral courage in joining the Resistance and facing deportation to a concentration camp, I was always afraid of him as a child and did not like him much. I felt guilty for feeling that way, but I sensed a deep and violent anger simmering under the surface that terrified me. My mother confessed she had the same feelings about him. Years later, my cousin Edy, Albert's daughter, told me that he used to punish her teenage infractions by forcing her naked under a cold shower and whipping her with his belt. When Edy decided to visit Mauthausen, she was surprised her father did not want to go along. But after that visit, she understood his reluctance and much more about him. While Edy became progressively estranged from her father because of his treatment of her, she knew that his behavior had roots in an experience of atrocities beyond her comprehension. While she was still angry at him and she no longer accepted any abuse from him, she felt she really could not judge him.

As I mourned my uncle's death, I felt that my old fear and anger toward him were transformed into deep sadness and compassion. And from that compassion, I felt an even greater resolve to keep addressing the costs of war.

Rita

From 1968 until his death in 1976, I was estranged from my father. He had been a loving parent who had helped me transition to life in the United States when I was six. I even entered college with the aspiration to become a medical doctor because he'd been a medic in the U.S. Army. But the father who returned in the summer of 1968 from his second tour of duty in Vietnam was not the father who raised me.

Unlike most people I knew in college, who were worried about the draft and demonstrating against the Vietnam War, I entered college the daughter of a veteran of the war, whose father had returned deeply changed. When he began to try to monitor my activities and friends the summer before I left for college, his cold, controlling behavior was a shock; he was dramatically different from the father who had warmly welcomed my friends into our home, trusted me to use good sense when I went out, and encouraged me to try new things. I decided not to live at home with my family anymore because I did not want to be in the same house with him. In refusing to capitulate to his constricting demands, I lost a major emotional support system, just as I was living away from home for the first time and entering the strange world of American college, a world both alienating and exciting.

The antiwar movement enabled me to move as far away from my father as possible. I became an antiwar activist without a deep understanding of why it was such a bad war—that understanding would take a long time to come. All through college, I lived a kind of double life with two very different, unintegrated parts. Many demonstrators demonized anyone in military service, and I was active in that movement and dated such activists. At the same time, I had a different circle of friends that included several veteran enlisted men who had fought in Vietnam. Though we never really discussed the details of their time there, the veterans were like many of the GIs I'd met and dated growing up on military bases. I liked their seriousness of purpose, their sense of honor and integrity, their sardonic humor, and their bluntness and lack of intellectual pretensions.

Until I immersed myself in trying to understand moral injury, I had not known the shocking events my father experienced in Vietnam that had changed him so much, events he could not possibly have explained to a teenage daughter. Though I had read books about the war, they did not help me understand the puzzle of why my father had changed. Only after I began this project on Soul Repair did I discuss his behavior with a cousin in Mississippi who had been close to my father. After she told me about what had happened to him near the end of his time in Vietnam, I started putting pieces together.

In the early years of the Vietnam War, my father was sent to work at the Landstuhl Army Medical Center in Germany, which is still the largest U.S. military facility outside the country. From 1963 until 1966, our family was stationed there, and both my father and I worked in the hospital where serious U.S. medical casualties from Vietnam were sent. My father worked as a professional medic; I worked as a volunteer "candy striper"; the name came from the pastel-striped, starched uniforms we wore. At the time, I thought I was having an exciting grown-up adventure that would prepare me for a career; I don't think I even knew there was a war going on. But my father must have known, and he must have learned a great deal about treating war wounds. In 1966, he got orders to report to Fort Irwin, California, to train for Vietnam.

I was shocked that my father had to go to war. He was so much older than the other soldiers, nearly forty-five—too old to be in a war. But my feelings about war were mixed with the excitement of moving to California, which we only knew from Hollywood movies. My father left for Vietnam in 1966, after the huge surge in troops began in 1965, to run a field medical aid station. We had gotten my father a portable cassette tape recorder and a box of blank tapes, so we could send messages back and forth. It was the last thing he packed the night before he left, and he made me promise to send him messages.

Tapes from my father arrived about every two weeks. As soon as I came home from school, I would check the dining table to see if one had arrived. Usually, there was one for me and one for my mother. We listened to the tapes privately in our own rooms, and then recorded over them with our messages. It saved money to reuse the tapes, but now I realize I have nothing left of the many messages my father sent me. I only have what I can remember and a few photographs. I know he once had to do an emergency appendectomy. We received a large envelope full of photos when he took his rest and recuperation (R&R) break in Japan with my mother's family. My teenaged male cousins, who had been toddlers when we left, thought he was cool, and the photos show them wearing his military hat and shirt, while he is in civilian clothes. He looked relaxed and happy, and he spoke warmly about his time there.

Now, I ponder what it meant for him, as a war veteran sent to occupied Japan, to marry a Japanese woman with a two-year-old daughter, who had been abandoned by the father of her child. I know he had a deep commitment to our well-being and was both a good father and husband. I wonder if he and many of his fellow veterans married Japanese nationals as a way to repair something the war had broken in them. Perhaps they sought some basic humanity that got lost in the demonization of Japanese people and the horrors of war. My Japanese grandfather liked Roy Brock a great deal and believed "he had a good heart," which might be one way to describe a war veteran with moral injury.

When my father returned home after a year in Vietnam, he decided to volunteer for a second tour, which infuriated my mother. She could not understand why he wanted to return to the war. He was in his twenty-eighth year of military service, and he had been planning to retire after thirty years of service. She did not want him to take the risk of being killed when he'd done his duty and was so close to getting out. Today, I understand why he went back—for his unit, his men.

His second tour began just before the Tet Offensive in January 1968, which was a turning point in the war. Six weeks later, CBS news anchor Walter Cronkite announced it was an unwinnable war. My father's tapes told me about a young Vietnamese woman, close to my age. In his spare time, my father filled his pack with medical supplies and hiked to Vietnamese villages to offer medical help. The young woman acted as his guide and as his interpreter in the villages. He described treating festering wounds, giving out penicillin and aspirin, doing some minor surgical procedures, and splinting broken limbs.

When I received those tapes, I just thought my father was being nice, doing a little extra to save a few more lives. Because he described a young woman who was also Asian, I imagined that she looked like me. Somehow, I found it comforting that he had her company there. I now have a better understanding of what it meant for him to be taking care of Vietnamese civilians, who might have been suspected insurgents. Like Kevin Benderman and Camilo Mejía, he made a decision to see the people in country as human beings and perhaps, in my father's case, human beings who looked like his own family at home. When a soldier starts to see the humanity of his enemies, he starts to pull away from the emotional cohesion of his unit and its aggression against the enemy, but this act of conscience can have unintended consequences. In my father's case, he may have put a young woman at risk by bringing her in regular proximity to his unit. I cannot imagine what he felt when he found the young woman's tortured body: perhaps guilt that he might have put her in harm's way, disgust and fury at the men who tortured and killed her, grief and shame at every-thing that had been destroyed.

I do not believe he ever recovered. He refused to stay in the military when he got home, but he returned to a family that had changed and moved on with life without him, so little of his old life remained. He made a huge effort to reconstruct a life, but I did not make that easy for him. Like him, I left and refused to look back, even when my father tried to apologize for his behavior to our family one Christmas. In 1976, he died of a heart attack while I was living in Switzerland. I think he died of a broken heart.

The past two years of work on moral injury have forced me to look back with new eyes. I now see in my father what I have seen in the many veterans I have worked with since we started this work, not just those we discuss but also many other men and women who testified in New York, attended our lectures and work-shops on moral injury, and wrote to us. I see in them and in my father remarkable human beings with good hearts who sought a better life and a life of purpose beyond their immediate world. They are people who sustained moral conscience within a system designed to compromise and even destroy it. My father was able to reach across the walls of socially constructed enmity and to offer love to people he had been taught to hate. I see in myself and in my moral commitments much of him, and I miss him now very much.

KEVIN BENDERMAN WONDERED why he was carrying a gun around in the Garden of Eden, and Joshua Casteel realized he was wearing Caesar's body armor and carrying an M-16 in Iraq, while denying he had been sent to kill people. Kevin had been in the area between the Tigris and Euphrates in Iraq, and a part-time preacher stationed with U.S. Defense staff told him that the area had once been the site of the Hanging Gardens of Babylon and even perhaps the original location of the Garden of Eden. Kevin noticed how lush and green the land was, how even stray kernels of corn accidentally scattered on the ground grew thick and tall in the fertile soil. He thought if any place could be the original Eden, Iraq might be it.

The Garden of Eden story describes human life as companionship between male and female in a well-watered, fertile garden. Situated on earth near four great rivers, including the Tigris and Euphrates of Iraq, the Garden of Eden also contained the dangers of evil inherent in life on earth. To guard against those dangers, clear boundaries were set for the still-naïve, first humans: they were not to touch or eat of the tree of knowledge about good and evil. By eating of that forbidden tree, they wanted knowledge they could not handle, like young soldiers who go to war imagining it as a personal test of their prowess, a video game, or a movie. When their eyes are opened by the knowledge they sought, Adam and Eve realize they are naked in their foolishness, and aware of their failure, they try to hide from the consequences. When called to account, they seek to dodge responsibility by claiming they are victims of trickery. Adam blames Eve, and she blames the serpent, but the damage is done. They have failed the test of moral discernment and responsibility. They are cursed with enmity and hardship and cast out of the garden to fend for themselves, because, lacking wisdom and unable to take responsibility for their power, they have become a danger to life itself. To prohibit their return to the Garden, an angel with a flaming sword guards the gate. Outside that gate are fratricide, war, empire, slavery, misogyny, and myriad forms of oppression.

When we violate our core moral values and fail to take responsibility, our moral conscience takes up that fierce flaming sword and guards what is left of our moral identity. To reenter the Garden, humanity must face that fierce angel. Unless the struggle is attempted, there is no way back and no way to know what remains in the garden behind the gate. The attempt to regain entry requires accepting responsibility for what we have done, but doing so may cost people their lives if they have to go back alone. Societies that launch wars, believing that weapons of death and destruction are noble, good, and lifesaving, or that wars are holy, do so dishonestly, without wisdom or the capacity to take moral responsibility for the harm they do, not just to their enemies, but to all they send into the maws of killing. We should not expect those who return to have to face that angel alone.

Few major social institutions teach moral integrity, courage, personal discipline, humility, a sense of purpose and responsibility, and commitment to the lives of others better than the armed services. And none works so thoroughly to compromise, deny, dismantle, and destroy the very values it teaches. This is the paradox of war. The human beings we know and care about volunteer for military service. We send them off to war, and they return morally injured. They still belong to us, they are still the people we love, and we cannot build a different humanity or different world without facing that fierce angel of moral injury together.

Veterans need each other, and they may never share with the rest of us what they share with each other. But they also need the civilians in their lives, those of us with whom they must learn to live again. To listen to veterans requires patience with their silence and with the confusion, grief, anger, and shame it carries. We must be willing to listen carefully without judgment and without a personal agenda. We must understand that respect for veterans requires us not to patronize them by trying to be their therapists—we do not hold the key to their redemption. It is not for us to forgive them but to help them find ways to forgive themselves and to let them know their lives mean something to us and to others. Finally, we must be willing to engage their moral and theological questions with openness and to journey with them as we are mutually transformed in the process.

Many religious communities have historical traditions that have long understood the suffering of soldiers and the moral transgressions that threaten souls, not just in the individual but also in the whole community. Traditions too focused on judgment and punishment of wrong doers or too facile in answering core questions about evil offer little and can even aggravate moral injury. But people of faith who are willing to wade into the complex moral questions of war and social responsibility and discern the meaning of spiritual life after war can engage the conversations that matter deeply and, in doing so, save lives.

Through our work on moral injury and the friendship of many veterans, we understand much more clearly and deeply how war has affected our lives, but we hope this book will not just make things in the past clearer. We seek a society that can understand that war and its aftermaths belong to all of us and are our responsibility. We believe that understanding moral injury can move our society into a different future. We seek a future that sustains our society's soul, the empathy and moral conscience that sustain our humanity. We seek a society that faces danger by holding sacred the difficult assembling of meaning, the respect for truth, the alliance of heart and mind, and the construction of life-sustaining relationships so injured by war. And we know that with the help and commitment of many, we can face the fierce angel and make this future possible.

Acknowledgments

We are deeply grateful for the generosity of the veterans whose stories are told in this book. Their willingness to share their struggles with moral injury and their honesty, courage, and generosity have made this work possible. It is our hope that their experiences will be of value to other veterans who live with moral injury and to all who love them.

We learned about moral injury through our work on the Truth Commission on Conscience in War (TCCW), and we thank everyone who made it happen, especially Ian Slattery, who did much of the organizing work and outreach to veterans and prepared witnesses to testify. In addition to those veterans mentioned in this book, we appreciate the testimony at the public hearing of veterans Jake Diliberto and Logan Mehl-Laituri and of Gold Star Mother Celeste Zappala. Other testifiers included Douglas Krantz, Nurah-Rosalie Amat'ullah, J. E. McNeil, Jonathan Shay, and Chris Hedges. We are indebted to Kaia Stern for chairing the entire four-hour hearing and to the multireligious group of chaplains who supported everyone at the hearing. We owe special thanks to the Riverside Church in New York City and its staff, especially Carol Nixon, for hosting the public hearing; to the Poverty Initiative at Union Theological Seminary in New York and

Charon Hribar for research and office and volunteer support; to Erin Reece and Betty-Jeanne Rueters-Ward for organizing work in New York; to Catherine Ryan and Gary Weimberg of Luna Productions for financial and on-the-ground support; and to Jo Ann Brock, who provided graphic artwork. Extraordinary institutional help was offered by Luna Productions and the Starr King School for the Ministry in Berkeley, California, and by Faith Voices for the Common Good in Oakland. Rebecca Parker and Joseph F. Terino assisted in New York, and Justin Waters created our first website. Jennifer Butler and the media staff at Faith in Public Life provided invaluable outreach to the press, not only for the New York hearing but also for a November 2010 press conference in Washington, D.C., where the TCCW report was released.

In the spring of 2010, a dozen college and graduate students from Hawaii to Connecticut, including several veterans, participated in a course we taught to prepare for the TCCW and produced excellent briefing materials for the seventy-five commissioners, as well as serving as commissioners in New York. Of that group, Miriam Marton also provided pro bono legal research and Jennifer Whitten expertly edited the final Commission Report. In addition, Pat Clark of the Greensboro Truth Commission and Peter Storey of the South Africa Truth and Reconciliation Commission provided invaluable advice to our class about truth commissions as we prepared for the hearing.

The TCCW report was released in November 2010 in Washington, D.C., at a press conference and at an Interfaith Service at National City Christian Church, which also hosted a conference on selective conscientious objection. We thank everyone who participated and made those events possible, many of whom were also at the events in New York, in particular, Betsy Eggert, Marinetta Cannito Hjort, James A. Forbes Jr., Ray McGovern, J. E. McNeil, and David B. Miller. Additional thanks go to Evelyn Hanneman, Mpho Tutu, Jordan Blevins, Bob Cooke, Mike Neuroth, Daisy Machado, and the extraordinary St. Camillus Multicultural Choir.

The first conference we held on moral injury in March 2011 in Berkeley was hosted by the Graduate Theological Union and First

Congregational Church of Berkeley, and ably administered by Irene Boczek. VA clinicians Shira Maguen and Kent Drescher, experts on moral injury, spoke, and Herman Keizer, Camilo Mejía, Abdullah bin Hamid Ali, Steve Jacobs, Lissette Larson-Miller, and Tyler Boudreau testified. In addition to the veterans mentioned here, we also have had the privilege of working with many others, too numerous to list individually, but particular thanks for special help go to Josh Stieber, India Drew, and Daniel Lakemacher.

Our work on moral injury will continue via the new Soul Repair Center at Brite Divinity School in Fort Worth, Texas, begun through a generous grant from the Lilly Endowment, Inc. The creation of this center is the culmination of two years of work, supported by Rebecca Parker, Kathleen Hurty, Bob Hill, Herman Keizer, Amir Soltani, JoAnne Kagiwada, Jim Eller, Craig Dykstra, Newell Williams, Tamara Rodenburg, Nancy Ramsay, Beverly Cotton, and the Brite faculty. Throughout this work, including at each of the events we planned, we have been sustained by the volunteer catering services of Stuart Fabregas, as well as his moral support, good company, and nourishing meals through the writing process. He was ably assisted by Stella, yellow lab extraordinaire, who protected us, kept us company, and entertained us.

We are especially grateful to our wonderful, astute editor at Beacon Press, Amy Caldwell, who has believed in this book and assisted enormously in its completion. Finally, we thank our families for telling us about their experiences of war and about the legacy of moral injury that has affected us all and for giving permission to tell those stories in this book.

Notes

Quotations from veterans were gathered by the authors through personal interviews and e-mail correspondence unless otherwise noted with a citation to the source. All quotations not cited are published here with permission.

INTRODUCTION

1. Rita Brock's talk "The Humanity of Soldiers" was given at the Rothko Chapel in Houston on April 12, 2011. For stories of Hunt's suicide, see Kristine Galvan, "Marine Loses Battle with PTSD," MyFox Houston, April 9, 2011, http://www.myfoxhouston.com; Kimberly Hefling, "Veteran Advocate Kills Self After War Tours," April 15, 2011, Associated Press, http://abcnews.go.com; James Dao, "Veteran Loses Battle With Depression After Helping Others With Their Own," April 15, 2011, *New York Times*, http://atwar.blogs.nytimes.com.

2. K. H. Seal et al., "Bringing the War Back Home: Mental Health Disorders among 103,788 US Veterans Returning from Iraq and Afghanistan Seen at Department of Veterans Affairs Facilities," *Archives of Internal Medicine* 167 (2007): 476–82.

3. Lisa M. Shin, Scott L. Rauch, and Roger K. Pitman, "Amygdala, Medial Prefrontal Cortex, and Hippocampal Function in PTSD," *Annals of the New York Academy of Sciences* 1071 (July 2006): 67–79; Katie Drummond, "Blasts to the Head 'Primed' Brains for PTSD, Study Says,"

Danger Room, February 22, 2012, http://m.wired.com; Judith Herman, *Trauma and Recovery: The Aftermath of Violence—from Domestic Abuse to Political Terror* (New York: Basic Books, 1992).

4. Tyler E. Boudreau, *Packing Inferno: The Unmaking of a Marine* (Port Townsend, WA: Feral House, 2008), 212.

5. Ibid., 220–21.

6. Jess Goodell and John Hearn, *Shade It Black: Death and After in Iraq* (Havertown, PA: Casemate Publishers, 2011); Brett T. Litz et al., "Moral Injury and Moral Repair in War Veterans: A Preliminary Model and Intervention Strategy," *Clinical Psychology Review* 29, no. 8 (2009): 695–706. See also Kent Drescher et al., "An Exploration of the Viability and Usefulness of the Construct of Moral Injury in War Veterans," *Traumatology* 17, no. 1 (March 2011): 8–13, http://tmt.sagepub.com.

7. Maureen Trudelle, *Navajo Lifeways: Contemporary Issues, Ancient Knowledge* (Oklahoma City: University of Oklahoma Press, 2001), 226. The U.S. National Library of Medicine, Bethesda, MD, describes the VA support and Navajo uses of the Enemy Way at their website in "Native Heritage: Traditions Preserved and Renewed," http://www.nlm.nih .gov. Bernard J. Verkamp, *The Moral Treatment of Returning Warriors in Early and Modern Times* (Chicago: University of Scranton Press, 2006), 1-8.

8. Video of veteran testimonies, a history, and the commission's report can be found at *Truth Commission on Conscience in War*, http://conscience inwar.org.

CHAPTER 1

1. Chuck Leddy, "A Critical Look at the GI Bill's Impact," *Boston Globe*, September 12, 2009, http://articles.boston.com; Sarah Turner and John Bound, "Closing the Gap or Widening the Divide: The Effects of the G.I. Bill and World War II on the Educational Outcomes of Black Americans," *Journal of Economic History* 63, no. 1 (March 2003): 145–77.

2. See "Small Towns Absorb the Toll of War," National Public Radio, February 20, 2007, http://www.npr.org; "Military Recruitment 2008: A Look at Age, Race, Income and Education of New Soldiers," *National Priorities Project*, February 18, 2009, http://nationalpriorities.org; "US Military Sees Surge in Asian-American Recruits: Education Opportunities, Increased Visibility Lure New Generation," Voice of America,

July 14, 2010, http://www.voanews.com; "Soldiers of Misfortune: U.S. Violations of the Optional Protocol on the Involvement of Children in Armed Conflict," American Civil Liberties Union, http://www.aclu.org.

3. Sgt. Kevin Benderman, with Monica Benderman, *Letters from Fort Lewis Brig: A Matter of Conscience* (Guilford, CT: Lyons Press, 2007): xvii.

4. Boudreau, *Packing Inferno*, 12, 128.

CHAPTER 2

1. Samuel Lyman Atwood Marshall, *Men Against Fire: The Problem of Battle Command* (New York: William Morrow, 1947), 79.

2. Material for this section is drawn from personal writing by Camillo "Mac" Bica sent to the authors in e-mails, as well as his testimony for the Truth Commission on Conscience in War (TCCW), http://conscience inwar.org.

3. Gary Weimberg and Catherine Ryan, *Soldiers of Conscience*, USA, 2007.

4. Camilo Mejía, *Road from Ar Ramadi: The Private Rebellion of Staff Sergeant Camilo Mejía* (Chicago: Haymarket Books, 2008), 138–39.

5. Ibid., 140.

6. Joshua Casteel, *Letters from Abu Ghraib* (New York: Essay Press, 2008), 4.

7. "Former Abu Ghraib Interrogator, Joshua Casteel, Interviewed," *Live-Leak*, August 8, 2007, http://www.liveleak.com.

8. Russ Bynum, "Images Behind Soldier's Iraq Refusal," Associated Press, January 17, 2004, http://www.commondreams.org.

9. David Zucchino, "Breaking Ranks to Shun War," *Los Angeles Times*, February 7, 2005, http://articles.latimes.com; Kevin Benderman, "A Matter of Conscience," AntiWar.com, January 18, 2005.

10. Boudreau, *Packing Inferno*, 175.

11. Colonel Westhusing's suicide note is found in Robert Bryce, "I am Sullied—No More: Faced with the Iraq War's Corruption, Col. Ted Westhusing Chose Death Before Dishonor," *Texas Observer*, March 8, 2007, http://www.texasobserver.org/.

CHAPTER 3

1. Chris Hedges and Laila Al-Arian, *Collateral Damage: America's War Against Iraqi Civilians* (New York: Nation Books, 2008), 112–13.

2. "Godspeed Clay Hunt," *Blackfive*, April 4, 2011, http://www.blackfive
   .net.

3. Lindsay Wise, "Marine Who Pushed Suicide Prevention Took Own Life:
   War Casualty on the Home Front," *Houston Chronicle*, April 9, 2011,
   http://www.chron.com.

4. Chris Hedges, *War Is a Force That Gives Us Meaning* (New York: Anchor
   Books, 2003), 38–39.

5. Chris Hedges, "War Is a Force That Gives Us Meaning," *Amnesty International NOW*, Winter 2002, http://www.thirdworldtraveler.com.

6. Stanley Milgram, *Obedience to Authority: An Experimental View* (New
   York: Harper Collins, 1974).

7. Peter A. French, *War and Moral Dissonance* (New York: Cambridge University Press, 2001), 157.

8. C. C. Bica, postwar journals, 1970, provided to the authors.

9. Mejía, *Road from Ar Ramadi*, 203.

10. Ibid., 205.

11. Ibid., 207.

12. Ibid., 213.

13. Ibid., 223.

14. Weimberg, *Soldiers of Conscience*.

15. Ibid.

16. Sgt. Kevin Benderman, "Truth Be Told," January 01, 2006, http://jack
    -dalton.blogspot.com; unpublished material from a personal interview
    with the authors, March 28, 2012.

17. Boudreau, *Packing Inferno*, 148.

18. Ibid., 207.

19. Ibid.

20. Ibid.

CHAPTER 4

1. "Evan Thomas and Sebastian Junger: Author One-on-One," Amazon
   .com, May 2010, http://www.amazon.com.

2. Boudreau, *Packing Inferno*, 79–80, 83; Tyler Boudreau, "Digging In,"
   Psychatrix, May 3, 2010, http://www.tylerboudreau.com/.

3. Boudreau, "Digging In."

4. Benderman, *Letters from Fort Lewis Brig*, 40.

5. Ibid., 45.

6. Quotations from his speeches at the Exploring Moral Injury Conference, Graduate Theological Union, Berkeley, CA, March 18–19, 2011, and published in Camilo E. Mejía, "Healing Moral Injury: A Lifelong Journey," *Fellowship of Reconciliation*, http://forusa.org/.

7. Christopher Clair, "Joshua Casteel," Be Remarkable series, University of Iowa website, October 19, 2009, http://www.uiowa.edu.

CHAPTER 5

1. George W. Casey Jr., "Comprehensive Soldier Fitness: A Vision for Psychological Resilience in the U.S. Army," *American Psychologist* 66, no. 1 (January 2011): 1–3.

2. Kenneth I. Pargament and Patrick J. Sweeney, "Building Spiritual Fitness in the Army," *American Psychologist* 66, no. 1 (January 2011): 59–60.

3. Department of the Army, "The Army Health Promotion Program," *Spiritual Fitness*, September 1, 1987, http://www.militaryatheists.org/regs/ArmyPam600–63–12v1987.pdf.

4. Suicide rates in the active duty military and veterans are discussed in Margaret C. Harrell and Nancy Berglass, "Losing the Battle: The Challenge of Military Suicide," Policy Brief of the Center for a New American Security, http://www.cnas.org; citation from "Why Does the Army Need Comprehensive Soldier Fitness?" *Comprehensive Soldier Fitness, Frequently Asked Questions*, http://csf.army.mil.

5. ABC news interview, August 21, 2011, http://abcnews.go.com.

6. Elizabeth Weill-Greenberg, "You May Be Asked to Do Things Against Your Beliefs," in *10 Excellent Reasons Not to Join the Military*, Elizabeth Weill-Greenberg, ed. (New York: The New Press, 2006), 119. A number of versions of "Sniper Wonderland" can be found online at YouTube, and the lyrics of two versions are posted at *Army Study Guide*, http://www.armystudyguide.com.

7. Jim Rendon, "Post-Traumatic Stress's Surprisingly Positive Flip Side," *New York Times Magazine*, March 22, 2012, http://www.nytimes.com.

8. Renato Rosaldo, *Culture and Truth: The Remaking of Social Analysis* (Boston: Beacon Press, 1989), 69–70.

9. Linda Hutcheon, "Irony, Nostalgia, and the Postmodern," University of Toronto English Library, January 19, 1998, http://www.library.utoronto.ca.

10. Edward Tick, "Healing the Wounds of War: Atonement Practices for Veterans," in *Beyond Forgiveness: Reflections on Atonement,* Phil Cousineau, ed. (San Francisco: Jossey-Bass, 2011), 123.

11. Ibid., 124.

12. Camillo "Mac" Bica, "Remembering the Context of War Crimes: The Crime of War Itself," *Truthout,* February 25, 2012, http://www.truth-out.org.

13. Norman Solomon, "In Praise of Kevin Benderman," Antiwar.com, July 30, 2005.

14. Camilo Mejía, "Concluding Remarks by Camilo Mejía," in *Winter Soldier: Iraq and Afghanistan, Eyewitness Accounts of the Occupations,* Iraq Veterans Against the War and Aaron Glantz, eds. (Chicago: Haymarket Books, 2008), 214–15.

15. Tyler Boudreau, "The Morally Injured," *Massachusetts Review* (Fall-Winter 2011–2012): 751, 753–54 .

16. Primo Levi, *The Drowned and the Saved* (New York: Vintage Books, 1989), 48–49.

Resources for Further Study

Barry, Kathleen. *Unmaking War, Remaking Men. How Empathy Can Reshape Our Politics, Our Soldiers and Ourselves.* Santa Rosa, CA: Phoenix Rising Press, 2011.

Benderman, Sgt. Kevin, with Monica Benderman. *Letters from Fort Lewis Brig: A Matter of Conscience.* Guilford, CT: Lyon's Press, 2007.

Bica, Camillo "Mac." "A Therapeutic Application of Philosophy. The Moral Casualties of War: Understanding the Experience." *International Journal of Applied Philosophy* 13, no. 1 (Spring 1999): 81–92.

————. "Law, Morality and Conscience in War." *Truthout.* Op-ed. March 1, 2010. http://archive.truth-out.org.

————. "The Invisible Wounds of War." *OpEdNews.* October 9, 2011. http://www.opednews.com.

————. "Remembering the Context of War Crimes: The Crime of War Itself." *Truthout.* Op-ed. February 25, 2012. http://www.truth-out.org.

Boudreau, Tyler. "Digging In." *Psychatrix.* May 3, 2010. http://www.tylerboudreau.com.

————. "The Morally Injured." *Massachusetts Review* (Fall-Winter 2011–2012): 746–54. http://www.massreview.org.

Boudreau, Tyler E. *Packing Inferno: The Unmaking of a Marine.* Port Townsend, WA: Feral House, 2008.

Bowden, Lisa, and Shannon Cain. *Powder: Writing by Women in the Ranks, from Vietnam to Iraq.* Tucson, AZ: Core Press, 2008.

Capps, Walter H., *The Unfinished War: Vietnam and the American Conscience.* Boston: Beacon Press, 1990.

Casteel, Joshua. *Letters from Abu Ghraib.* Ithaca, NY: Essay Press, 2008.

Delgado, Aidan. *The Sutras of Abu Ghraib.* Boston: Beacon Press, 2008.

Fassin, Didier, and Richard Rechtman. *The Empire of Trauma: An Inquiry into the Condition of Victimhood.* Rachel Gomme, trans. Princeton, NJ: Princeton University Press, 2009.

French, Peter A. *War and Moral Dissonance.* New York: Cambridge University Press, 2001.

Glantz, Aaron, and Iraq Veterans Against the War, eds. *Winter Soldier: Iraq and Afghanistan: Eyewitness Accounts of the Occupations.* Chicago: Haymarket Books, 2008.

Goodell, Jessica, with John Hearn. *Shade It Black: Death and After in Iraq.* Haverton, PA: Casemate Books, 2011.

Grossman, Dave. *On Killing: The Psychological Cost of Learning to Kill in War and Society.* New York: Little, Brown, 1995.

Hedges, Chris. *War Is a Force That Gives Us Meaning.* New York: Anchor Books, 2003.

Hedges, Chris, and Laila Al-Arian. *Collateral Damage: America's War Against Iraqi Civilians.* New York: Nation Books, 2008.

Herman, Judith. *Trauma and Recovery: The Aftermath of Violence—from Domestic Abuse to Political Terror.* New York: Basic Books, 1992.

Jamail, Dahr. *The Will to Resist: Soldiers Who Refuse to Fight in Iraq and Afghanistan.* Chicago: Haymarket Books, 2009.

Levi, Primo. *The Drowned and the Saved.* Raymond Rosenthal, trans. New York: Vintage Books, 1989.

Lifton, Robert J. *Home from the War.* New York: Simon and Schuster, 1973.

Litz, Brett T., et al. "Moral Injury and Moral Repair in War Veterans: A Preliminary Model and Intervention Strategy. *Clinical Psychology Review* 29, no. 8 (2009): 695–706.

Marlantes, Karl. *What It Is Like to Go to War.* New York: Atlantic Monthly Press, 2011.

Marshall, Samuel Lyman Atwood. *Men Against Fire: The Problem of Battle Command.* New York: William Morrow, 1947.

Mejía, Camilo. *Road from ar Ramadi: The Private Rebellion of Staff Sergeant Camilo Mejía*. New York: The New Press, 2007.

Mejía, Camilo E. "Healing Moral Injury: A Lifelong Journey." *Fellowship of Reconciliation*. http://forusa.org.

Rockwood, Lawrence. *Walking Away from Nuremberg: Just War and the Doctrine of Command Responsibility*. Amherst, MA: University of Massachusetts Press, 2007.

Shay, Jonathan. *Achilles in Vietnam: Combat Trauma and the Undoing of Character*. New York: Scribner, 1984.

————. *Odysseus in America: Combat Trauma and the Trials of Homecoming*. New York: Scribner, 2002.

Sherman, Nancy. *The Untold War: Inside the Hearts, Minds, and Souls of Our Soldiers*. New York: W. W. Norton, 2010.

Sippola, John, Amy Blumenshine, Donald A. Tubesing, and Valerie Yancey. *Welcome Them Home–Help Them Heal: Pastoral Care and Ministry with Service Members Returning from War*. Duluth, MN: Whole Person Associates, 2009.

"Truth Commission on Conscience in War: Final Report." *Truth Commission on Conscience in War*. http://conscienceinwar.org.

Verkamp, Bernard J. *The Moral Treatment of Returning Warriors in Early Medieval and Modern Times*. Chicago: University of Scranton Press, 2006.

SELECTED FILMOGRAPHY

Amadei, Aureliano. *20 Cigarettes (Venti Sigarette)*. Italy, 2010.

Dick, Kirby. *The Invisible War*. United States, 2012.

Diritti, Giorgio. *The Man Who Will Come (L'Uomo Che Verrà)*. Italy, 2009.

Faulkrod, Patrice. *The Ground Truth: After the Killing Ends*. United States, 2006.

Gibney, Alex. *Taxi to the Dark Side*. United States, 2007.

Haggis, Paul. *In the Valley of Elah*. United States, 2007.

Hetherington, Tim, and Sebastian Junger. *Restrepo*. United States, 2010.

McLagan, Meg, and Daria Sommers. *Lioness*. United States, 2008.

Pierce, Kimberly. *Stop-Loss*. United States, 2008.

Rosi, Francesco. *Many Wars Ago (Uomini Contro)*. Italy, 1970.

Weimberg, Gary, and Catherine Ryan. *Soldiers of Conscience*. United States, 2007.

ADDITIONAL RESOURCES

Truth Commission on Conscience in War. http://conscienceinwar.org/.

"Geneva Conventions and Additional Protocols, 1949." International Committee of the Red Cross. http://www.icrc.org.

"Nuremberg Trial Proceedings." Yale Law School, Lillian Goldman Law Library. http://avalon.law.yale.edu.

"Operation Recovery." Iraq Veterans Against the War. http://www.ivaw.org.

The Soul Repair Center. Brite Divinity School. http://britesoulrepair.org.